Post-Romantic Stress Disorder

Post-Romantic Stress Disorder

WHAT TO DO WHEN THE HONEYMOON IS OVER

NEW DISCOVERIES ABOUT LUST, LOVE, AND SAVING YOUR MARRIAGE BEFORE IT'S TOO LATE

JOHN E. BRADSHAW

Health Communications, Inc.
Deerfield Beach, Florida

www.hcibooks.com

**Library of Congress Cataloging-in-Publication Data
is available through the Library of Congress**

© 2014 John E. Bradshaw

ISBN-13: 978-0-7573-1813-9 (paperback)
ISBN-10: 0-7573-1813-4 (paperback)
ISBN-13: 978-0-7573-1814-6 (ePub)
ISBN-10: 0-7573-1814-2 (ePub)

Publisher: Health Communications, Inc.
          3201 S.W. 15th Street
          Deerfield Beach, FL 33442–8190

Cover photo by Karen A. Bradshaw
Cover design by Larissa Hise Henoch
Interior design and formatting by Lawna Patterson Oldfield

To my courageous sister, Barbara Ann, and
my best friend and brother, Richard Allen (both deceased),
whose emotional wounds caused you to live alone
for a part of your lives. I love you dearly!

To my extraordinary and beautiful wife, Karen,
and to my children, John Jr. and Ariel, and my
stepchildren, Brad and Brenda. Thank you for giving
me your precious selves! I love you dearly!

CONTENTS

PART I

Mother Nature's Old Black Magic

Richard Burton, on first seeing
Elizabeth Taylor:

"She was famine, fire, destruction and plague . . .
the only true begetter. Her breasts were apocalyptic, they
would topple empires before they withered . . .
her body was a miracle of construction . . .
she was unquestionably gorgeous. She was lavish . . .
she was in short, too bloody much . . .
those huge violet blue eyes had an odd glint . . .
Aeons passed, civilizations came and went while these
cosmic headlights examined my flawed personality.
Every pockmark on my face became
a crater of the moon."

—As quoted in *Meeting Mrs. Jenkins*

PROLOGUE

As they got into bed, Paul snuggled up to his wife Shirley's back and then reached over to touch her breast. He had done this countless times during the year-and-a-half sexual phase of their courtship. It was the first ritual move that Paul used to initiate the foreplay they engaged in prior to their sexual interchange. Shirley had a clear and predictable response: she'd turn toward Paul, a signal that gave him "permission" to touch her other breast. This interactive foreplay had become more or less unconscious, a fairly automatic exchange between them that had a predictable but nonetheless enjoyable ending.

Paul and Shirley had been married a little over a month, still in the newlywed stage of their marriage. They had a robust sex life, and had mutually agreed that they'd only refrain from sexual activity if they were completely exhausted after a long day at work, or some form of physical exercise. So what happened next was a major departure from their routine, and took their relationship

4

down an unexpected path. Instead of turning toward Paul as she always did, Shirley tilted her head back and said, "Let's just cuddle tonight."

Paul was certainly not prepared for this. All day, he had looked forward to having sex. Shirley's response gave him a strong adrenaline rush and left him feeling like he had been punched in the gut. He felt like yelling, "You've been different since we got married!" Instead, he held his tongue and shut down, saying nothing. He abruptly moved back to his side of the bed. He lay there motionless, his muscles tight and his breathing shallow.

He thought about how vigorously sexual he and Shirley had been throughout their courtship. In the early days, they made love at least once a day. They couldn't get enough of each other. The sex Paul had with Shirley was truly "amazing," and she was often the initiator of their sexual routine, often suggesting new, experiential behavior. One day, she bought a porno DVD on her way home from work, which launched them into a wild night of passionate lovemaking and made them miss dinner altogether. Paul felt lucky he'd found a woman like Shirley. And now, this—just cuddling? Glaring at the ceiling, Paul blurted out, "What's the matter? Have I done something wrong?"

"There's absolutely nothing wrong, I'm just not in the mood," Shirley replied matter-of-factly. "Can we discuss this in the morning?" It was prudent of Shirley

to want to avoid a discussion about their sex life—or any other relationship issue—at 12:30 AM, but it just made Paul angrier. He lay there feeling paralyzed, and Shirley's rhythmic breathing let him know she had fallen asleep. Paul was still aroused and he began what can be a divisive practice in marriage: he relieved himself by masturbating.

Even though Shirley said she'd talk about what had happened the next day, neither of them brought it up. They just avoided it as though nothing had happened. But that single incident started a divisive pattern, and this scenario was repeated many times over the next two years. Three years later, they divorced at Paul's initiation. Shirley was deeply wounded by the divorce. Paul told his friends that Shirley had fallen out of love with him. He turned his energy to fantasy self-sex and two affairs. With his sexual desire directed elsewhere, he felt that he, in turn, had fallen out of love with Shirley.

Paul and Shirley are an example of a phenomena I call Post-Romantic Stress Disorder (PRSD). Almost every couple experiences some degree of Post-Romantic Stress. Those with a "good enough" attachment program, and with good enough self-esteem with relatively little baggage from the past, are generally able to work through this unexpected challenge without any scars.

Some with poor levels of selfhood do stay together, living with varying degrees of satisfaction. But only 50 percent of all marriages actually stay together, and of this 50 percent, 17 percent claim to be disappointed, unfulfilled, and unhappy. After counseling over 700 couples over a twenty-year span, it is my observation that only 15 percent are truly incompatible and the remaining 85 percent can achieve a "good enough," fulfilling marriage. The 50 percent divorced and those who are unhappily married are in the swoon of Post-Romantic Stress Disorder. I've seen an alarming number of people throw away perfectly decent marriage partners.

My major goal in this book is to offer you a compelling argument that will stop you from throwing away what may well be your perfectly good marriage partner or from ending a perfectly good relationship that seems stuck.

A secondary goal of this book is to offer you the latest biological and anthropological data relating to "being in-love," the experience of lust and being solidly attached to a love partner, a state that is the foundation for long-term, lasting love.

A final feature of this book is to present six new discoveries relating to falling "in-love" and staying in an ever-growing and deepening love.

In Part I, I will present you with the three newly discovered brain programs that govern our meeting and mating a partner and staying with them to produce an offspring. These help us to fully understand the fallacy of confusing sexual desire with true love. In Part II, I'll present three other new discoveries: the neuroplasticity of the brain, willpower as a "physical force," and the affect (feeling) system as the primary source of human behavior. These new discoveries can change any stuck relationship.

Finally, I need to remind the reader that I am a theologian, counselor, and teacher. I have three master degrees—one in theology, one in philosophy, and one in psychology. I spent four years of post-graduate work at Rice University. As I see it, my job is to synthesize the works of the true masters in the field of relationship health. These masters include people like: Virginia Satir, Murray Bowen, Milton Erickson, Richard Bandler, John Grinder, Leslie Cameron Bandler, Harriet Lerner, Pat Love, Pia Melody, Claudia Black, Pat Carnes, David Schnarch, Peter Levine, Bissel van der Kolk; and the most important for this book, Helen Fisher and Jeffrey Schwartz. Their work permeates this book. I thank them for their superb contributions. I take full responsibility for my interpretation of their work.

1

Who Taught You the Meaning of Love?

> *. . . There is the heat of Love, the pulsing*
> *rush of Longing, the lover's whisper, irresistible—*
> *magic to make the sanest man go mad.*
>
> —Homer, The Iliad

Everyone believes they know what love is. Unfortunately, the English language only has one word for "love." As I wrote in my book *Creating Love,* other languages, notably Greek and Latin, have many: *caritas* (love of God and humanity); *philos* (friendship, fondness); *eros* (erotic love); and *agape* (deep, mature love).

Eros is an innate, instinctual desire. *Eros,* as it is experienced by lovers in-love, is powerful because its biological purpose is to meet a suitable partner, to mate, and most often to produce offspring. Over a hundred studies have shown that over 50 percent of adults confuse *eros* (falling in-love) and *agape* (mature, soulful love). So when the majority of people speak about love, they usually have being "in-love" in mind.

Where do we learn about being in-love? Certainly not from our parents, who are no longer in-love, although they may pretend to be when they are around us. All too often we have grown up witnessing marital conflict, and sadly, many times our living models of marital love end up divorcing. According to the latest research, only 33 percent of those who are married are really happy. If this research is correct, it means that 67 percent of the population grew up experiencing faulty models of love. The divorce rate is so high partly because so many folks have no real knowledge of what mature love actually is and confuse it with the feeling of being in-love and having intense sexual desire.

It's now clear that mature love develops in distinct stages that require docility, patience, the willingness to compromise, and sometimes the necessity of going back and confronting what the Jungian therapist James Hollis calls our "hauntings." Mature love requires skills that many of the in-love lovers do not believe they need and simply refuse to learn. When you're in-love, everything comes naturally and spontaneously; you simply go with the blissful flow, and there's nothing you have to learn or *work* at.

Since we cannot really learn about being in-love from our parents, where do we learn about it? Often, our parents point to other couples as examples of love and intimacy. When I was growing up, we had neighbors that my mother cited as a couple with a fabulous marriage. To outsiders, perhaps, but behind closed doors it was another story. I hung out with their children and heard a lot of arguments and discord.

LOVE STORIES ARE JUST THAT . . . STORIES

Many of us learned about being in-love from books, mythology, movies, and television shows. While entertaining, these models are as inadequate as they are destructive.

Think about the following twelve movies:

The African Queen	*Pretty Woman*
The Bridges of Madison County	*Terms of Endearment*
Casablanca	*There's Something About Mary*
Dr. Zhivago	*Titanic*
The English Patient	*When Harry Met Sally*
French Kiss	*You've Got Mail*

Also, think of fairy tales like *Sleeping Beauty*, *Cinderella*, and so on. The list could go on for pages, and while the plot lines are all different, they all have one thing in common: they are love stories—with the emphasis on "stories." Some are profound, others fairly trite, and all fanciful. Still, we are drawn to them (at least I am) out of an idealistic longing for a carefree love utopia. We leave the theater feeling wistful and hopeful. There is always a happy ending. But these love stories have something else in common. These stories end before the *real* love process begins. Not one pair of the famous couples in our list of movies ever actually *live* together for any amount of time. We have a few notable movies or TV shows that deal with the beginning and middle years of marriage, but in most cases, we have no idea what would happen in the relationship if the toilet backed up, the roof caved in, the husband got fired, or the house went into foreclosure. We are not given the slightest idea of each couple's compatibility. We are yoked to a culture that is saturated with the rapture of courtship. Evolution expands by ever-increasing complexity and by its own unique kind of compatibility. Knowing this, then, it is frightening that our ideals about love and marriage come from fiction and imagination. They may also come from the movie stars who played the great lovers in movies.

I opened this book with a quote by Richard Burton about his first impressions of Elizabeth Taylor. They had one of the great onscreen and offscreen romances. However, their actual life together was more the stuff of a romantic nightmare rather than a dream. The movie that comes closest to their reality was probably *Who's Afraid of Virginia Woolf?* Definitely not a feel-good movie.

Love stories are just that—stories! It's a wonder to me that the divorce rate isn't far higher than it is, and it's clear why so many married people are unhappy. Without a clear vision of the self-generating stages that are involved in the growth of mature love, and without "working" on your *own* sense of self, you've got nothing to go on.

I counseled at least seven hundred couples over a twenty-year period. The most important thing I learned was that most of these couples were carrying unresolved issues from the past. Their unfinished business damaged their sense of self. Most had some degree of unresolved childhood abandonment, neglect, abuse, and enmeshment issues. These wounds caused spontaneous "age regressions" and emotional blocks, which were one major reason these couples could not deal with their differences or effectively resolve their conflicts. Their selves were *false selves*. As I described in my book *Bradshaw On: The Family*, people raised in dysfunctional homes "lose their solid self-esteem and develop a false self. As children they quickly learn that the way to get love is to give up their authentic self and instead develop a self that meets the demands of blind obedience and duty. When the core of self is covered up with a false self, true self-love and self-esteem are impossible."

Joel Covitz in his excellent book, *Emotional Child Abuse*, quotes one of his clients who said, "The way I knew my father loved me was when I was not being myself."

As adults in a relationship, their unresolved issues made their conflicts quite *childish*, and neither partner knew how to argue without shaming judgment and/or overstepping their own and their partner's boundaries. In most of their conflicts, they were in their childish ego state, constantly keeping score: who worked the hardest, who spent the most time with the children, who controlled the money, and which partner had done the most for the other.

I had two clients, both Ph.D.s, who vehemently argued over who deserved to get the green Christmas tree ornaments in their impending divorce! They tore each other up over something they only saw once a year. It was the epitome of childish behavior from two highly educated professionals.

Please note that I don't believe that I'm the judge and jury over my clients. I have had to grow up and repair my own developmental dependency need deficits (DDDs; these are needs that weren't fulfilled during the childhood years, and must be met in order for us to develop a solid sense of self and emotional literacy; we'll explore DDDs more fully in Chapter 8). I recently started a quarrel with my wife over her airline frequent flyer miles. I asserted that since I worked and got paid, the miles should go to me. My wife protested and said she was saving for a trip with her best friend. Suddenly, the lightbulb went off and I started laughing! I realized I was acting like a five-year-old, comparing who got the most (of whatever). My wife laughed, too. Our functional adults had taken over. The fact is neither one of us gives a squat about the frequent flyer miles—other than the fact that they save us money!

Think about some of your recent squabbles with your partner. Take a few minutes to jot them down—what were you fighting about? What was the big issue, and what did you want? Seeing them in black-and-white, I'll bet you'd find a couple of kids fighting over "who got the most" of something. The same childish immaturity comes up over and over again until we deal with our post-romantic stress disorder. Divorce courts are packed with adult children—adults with a wounded inner child living inside them—who then find another adult child, get married, and often wind up in divorce court. It's important that we realize that each of us may have an unrealistically arrested conception of love and romance. All adult children have a damaged and immature sense of self.

THE CENTURIES-OLD POWER OF "IN-LOVE"

Why do we now, and have for centuries past, hang on to a definition of love that is limited to "in-love" romance behaviors—especially the belief that *sexual desire* and *true love* go hand-in-hand? As you will see in what follows, the belief that when sexual desire ends, we are no longer in-love is a tremendously damaging belief that often leads to divorce and eats away at family health.

Let's not kid ourselves, however, about the compelling, longstanding power of the in-love belief. In her book *Why We Love*, anthropologist Helen Fisher writes, "The drive to fall in-love has produced some of humankind's most compelling operas, plays, and novels, our most touching poems and haunting melodies, the world's finest sculptures and paintings . . . romantic love has brought many of us tremendous joy."

2

Falling "In-Love" and the Amazing Sex That Goes with It

The brain is an incredible creation;
it begins working long before your birth and
doesn't stop until you fall in love.

—Pat Love, *The Truth About Love*

We owe to the Middle Ages the two worst
inventions of humanity—romantic
love and gunpowder.

—André Maurois

What is the "energy" that comes from the experience of being in-love? Why has it ensconced our global culture, motivating poets and artists with its profound beauty? And why does it have the potential power to ruin what could be perfectly good marriages and inflict intense suffering on seemingly emotionally healthy individuals? In what follows, I'll present the revolutionary new data on the *three primordial brain networks* that have evolved to direct and safeguard our meeting, mating, and reproduction. The findings explain the power of falling in-love, an innate drive that is part of the life force itself.

In this chapter, I will present some of the seemingly wild and crazy behaviors that are the markers of being in-love. The couples with which I've chosen to illustrate these behaviors are real people that I have counseled. Their names, certain elements of their personalities, and their surroundings have been changed. The details pertaining to their behavior are accurate. The couples I've chosen engaged in some interactions that go beyond the more or less normal profile of couples who are in-love. The exaggerations in this example offer a helpful way to illustrate the behaviors created by Mother Nature's old black magic.

TOM AND ALICE:
LOST IN A TEENAGE TIME MACHINE

I counseled a client, who I'll call Tom, over a three-and-a-half-year period. Tom had an in-love mate, who I'll call Alice. At the very start of their courtship, Tom told me he had a long telephone conversation with Alice that was so intoxicating it went on for more than five hours. Other than the occasional bathroom break, the conversation was unbroken, and even Tom was surprised that he hadn't noticed that so much time had passed until he hung up the phone and looked at the clock. A lot of the talk had been meandering and effulgent expressions of love. Tom said he couldn't find the words that truly expressed how he felt about Alice. He just kept repeating to her, "I love you," and Alice answered likewise.

This might sound like something that a couple of high school kids would do, but it's interesting to note that Tom was fifty-eight and Alice was thirty-two. While Alice was considerably younger than Tom—which they said wasn't an issue with either of them—she certainly wasn't an adolescent. Their relationship appeared to swallow them both into a vortex, where they regressed to teenage-like behavior. How and why did this happen? It is the chemicals triggered by the brain in-love.

Tom and Alice felt like soul mates, bound by an unseen cosmic force, and were amazed that they had similar experiences in their lives before they met. In reality, these were hardly amazing coincidences, and most of their similar experiences were downright ludicrous.

For instance, one day Alice expressed joy and astonishment that she had gone to high school and so had Tom! This was not the same high school, mind you, just high school in general. Only an in-love lover would find such a thing astonishing. On another occasion, Tom said, "I can't believe you like black molasses on your breakfast biscuits. I thought I'd never find anyone whose tastes were like mine!" Each of their families had gone to London on a summer vacation when they were twelve years old (although twenty-six years apart)! You can see the behavior pattern: lovers in-love think of similar experiences that happened prior to their meeting each other as signs that they were meant to be together—forever.

Both Tom and Alice had a great sense of humor. They were constantly joking and laughing with each other. A sense of humor is attractive to both sexes (usually more so for women). Alice's wry wit was one of the reasons Tom's attraction to Alice deepened his.

Then there were the physical attributes. At six feet, four inches tall, Tom's stature was physically commanding, and tall men are generally attractive to women. Alice told Tom she dreamed of having a tall man as a lover. Tom had a symmetrical face, with slightly taut jawbones. He was, however, somewhat plump with a bit of a protruding belly. Alice told Tom that his sturdy body and height made her feel extremely secure. Women are attracted to men who offer protection and security.

Tom and Alice were *madly* in-love. They were downright intoxicated by each other, drunk, out of their minds, as if they'd downed a fifth of vodka. Their attraction was potent and immediate. They'd met at a conference on financial planning. Tom was one of the presenters and caught Alice's eye while signing a new book he had recently written. The eye contact took Tom by surprise; he was there as an industry professional, not someone looking for love. They exchanged words—but their mutual gaze said a whole lot more. Tom immediately saw their age difference, but he felt a sense of urgency, like he couldn't leave the hotel without her. He asked his manager to get her phone number, something he had never done before.

After the conference where he met Alice, Tom had two more speaking engagements, then a planned fishing trip. He didn't get home for two weeks. A week after their first meeting, Tom's manager called with Alice's phone number. Tom felt exhilarated and alive, but wanted to wait until he got home to call Alice. He feared doing so, because of his age, and for fear that she might have no real romantic interest in him. The fear and risk of being rejected enhanced Tom's feeling of "desire" for her.

Alice later confessed that she fell in love with Tom while listening to his presentation. She loved his voice and his command of language. He had an authoritarian certainty about what he was saying. This triggered Alice's overall need for someone to provide financial and emotional security for her. Tom was at a loss to explain why he had fallen in-love with Alice.

When Tom returned home from his fishing trip he found a letter from Alice. In her note she said she would be in Dallas for a week—as it turned out, five days after he'd read the letter—and suggested they meet and have coffee. Tom was thrilled by this note. It made him feel alive and energized in a way he hadn't been in years. Because of their age difference, he was still fearful and slightly ashamed about the encounter, but he went anyway. When they met, Alice poured out warning secrets that were candid and shocking for a first date. First, she was divorced and had two small children, ages five and three. Also, she was being financially supported by a wealthy elderly man in her church. Finally, she told Tom she had herpes and padded her bra because she had extremely small breasts. Tom typically lusted after large-breasted women, but for some reason, he didn't care about Alice's chest size, and didn't think twice about the deception. In fact, none of the troubling things Alice divulged set off alarms in his head, or quelled the intensity of his desire for her.

They had intense sex on the first night they were together. It continued the next afternoon and all night long. Within four days of having "amazing" sex with Alice, Tom told me she was talking about marriage! Tom knew it was crazy and was certain he didn't want to get married again, but he went along with it.

THE REAL YOU

Over the next few months Tom and Alice looked at houses in their respective cities of residence. Alice lived in St. Paul, Minnesota, and Tom in Houston, Texas. When they were not actually having sex, they were totally focused on each other—talking and joking on the phone for some time every day. When they were together and not having sex, they kissed, touched, and focused their interest solely on each other. Emily Dickinson wrote a fine poem entitled, "I Have No Life but This":

I HAVE NO LIFE BUT THIS,
TO LEAD IT HERE;
NOR ANY DEATH, BUT LEST
DISPELLED FROM THERE;
NOR TIE TO EARTHS TO COME,
NOR ACTION NEW,
EXCEPT THROUGH THIS EXTENT,
THE REALM OF YOU.

This poem describes Tom and Alice, who were living in "the realm of you." Everything in both their lives was governed by the other's wants and perception of them.

Alice was talking about marriage before Tom had met her two children, and before she had met his grown-up children. Tom was okay with this because he was basically ashamed of his relationship with Alice (his biological son was only six years older than Alice). Alice didn't particularly care for St. Paul and was eager to move and get married, especially to someone in Tom's financial situation. He had a ranch in West Texas and several other properties. His wealth and power were a big turn-on to Alice.

While Alice was very proper—very religious—in her public persona, she had a shadow self that liked wild and downright uninhibited and lawless sex. Paradoxically, she put the quietus on intercourse after their first few wild sexual days together, saying that it should only take place after they were married. At the same time, she was voracious about oral sex and both were drawn to anal sex; Alice also reneged on her own rule of intercourse at unexpected times.

As Tom shared his love life with me, I began to see a vibrant picture of in-love romance, but I was also quite concerned that Alice might be emotionally troubled. Tom had originally come to me because of his co-dependency, a disease of the developing self. He had made great progress in strengthening his solid sense of self but I feared he was regressing. I invited them in for a counseling session. I strongly suggested that they slow down. I probed Alice about her vacillation between abstinence from normal sex until marriage, followed by episodes of uninhibited sexual intercourse and other behaviors. I questioned her about the old man who was supporting her. Tom defended any aspect of her behavior that I found inconsistent and manipulative. I got nowhere, reminding me of what the great therapist and writer James Hollis said: "You cannot do therapy with people who are in-love." They are drunk, out of their minds.

Tom was a hard-nosed, highly successful financial planner. He had a history of not being able to show his emotions, or even being in touch with them at all. This had been a major cause for his two failed marriages. He was very cerebral. Had this been a business deal, Tom would have done all the necessary due diligence and wouldn't have entered into a partnership with someone so duplicitous with terms that were so sketchy.

Still, in our counseling sessions, my warnings about Alice fell like water off a duck's back.

So Tom and Alice continued to have amazing sex for hours at a time, and when they were not together, they talked for hours on the phone, often reaching climax when they "talked dirty" (Tom's words) to each other. Tom's every waking thought was about Alice, or should I say *sex* with Alice. They both made surprise visits to each other, arriving late at night just to have sex with each other. It has been hypothesized that when the human brain is in the frenzied euphoria of "romantic love" it is saturated with the chemical phenylethylamine (PEA), an amphetamine-like neurotransmitter that has been found to release dopamine and norepinephrine, and both these neurotransmitters reduce serotonin. A reduction in serotonin can be a cause of obsessive thinking. This is why PEA has been called the "love drug" or the "love molecule."

What I will subsequently call the "PEA dopamine cocktail" also raises blood pressure and blood glucose levels. The result is that it makes lovers feel more energetic and alert. It gives them an amazing sense of energy, well-being, and contentment.

The brain saturated with the PEA dopamine cocktail (only a hypothesis prior to Fisher's work) explains why Tom and Alice could have long hours of actual sex, and the reduced serotonin helps explain why they obsessed about each other and talked for hours on the phone. The long hours were also due to their high levels of intelligence and their sense of humor. They made each other laugh a lot, which contributed to their feeling so good.

ENHANCED TESTOSTERONE

Most important, PEA elevates the testosterone that governs the sex drive. Alice and Tom's lovemaking for hours at a time was atypical for both of them. When people are in-love, their testosterone levels rise to atypical heights, only to return to their normal levels when the in-love "spell" wears off.

Besides making lovers feel powerful and unquenchably optimistic, PEA is enhanced by adversity, fear, danger, distance, secrecy, and risk. The geographic distance between Alice and Tom was not a burden; it actually enhanced the intensity of their desire for each other.

As I mentioned, Tom was somewhat overweight when he met Alice. As their time together progressed, he lost weight without even trying. Alice confessed that she was normally not very sexual (actually had a certain disdain for men). One night, when Tom was visiting Alice in Minnesota, he found her diary open on her bed stand. Tom looked at the page it was open to, which read, "When I'm in complete control, I may never have sex again." According to Tom, Alice's alcoholic father lived as a nudist when he was at home. Alice was both shocked and, when she reached puberty, aroused by his nudity. According to Alice, her mother found her husband disgusting, and humiliated and shamed him frequently.

Tom's friends, who were in his age group, thought he was out of his mind because of the age difference with Alice, and moreover because she was somewhat plain-looking and lacked a certain sophistication. This made Tom conceal his time with

Alice from his children and friends, and also to distance himself from them. This is often a trait of lovers in-love. They want their beloved and no one else. Their relationship is "special" and "exclusive." They are perfectly happy to be alone.

Men generally have more testosterone than women, and men and women are stimulated by different things. Alice, for example, became highly aroused if Tom dominated her and called her by demeaning sexual words. When Tom role played with Alice and said she was a little slut, a "bad" girl who only wanted sex, Alice neared climax by just hearing the words. My guess was that, at an early age, she had identified with her mother's disgust of sex in general and her father in particular. Disgust, shame, and humiliation turned her on. Conquest can be a natural turn-on for both men and women, but for Alice it was shameful and degraded conquest that aroused her. Tom and Alice could play either part, the cruel conqueror or the degraded victim.

Alice was also turned on by what commonly turns women on sexually: romantic words, images, and rituals of affection. She especially liked love letters, chocolate candy (which contains phenylethylamine), endearing conversations, elegant dinners, and poetry. Women and men are often aroused by their lover's smell and the sound of their voice. Alice loved Tom's scent. Tom would listen to Alice's recorded voice on her answering machine over and over again when he could not talk to her personally.

Both sexes are excited sexually by visual stimuli (more so for men). Despite her lack of pulchritude and fleshy breasts, Alice

did have an ample derriere. According to Tom, Alice loved to
dress in a way that showed off her backside. When men fantasize, they too often conjure up vivid images of body parts. This
is why pornography, cybersex, and strip bars are so desired by
men.

I'll end this chapter by summing up the salient elements
that constitute this initial in-love stage of romance. The following seem to be universal markers of most people's feelings and
behaviors when they are in-love:

OTHERATION: A word used by the Spanish philosopher José
    Ortega y Gasset. He contrasts "otheration" with living
    from within. All animals are "otherated"; they live in a
    state of outward vigilance, endlessly looking for food—
    lovers are obsessively focused on each other, living in "the
    realm of you." Each partner has a focused and compul-
    sive interest in every detail related to the other, the world
    of "you."

DESTINY: Lovers experience the in-love state as part of each
    one's destiny. The love one has for the other is beyond
    their shallow choices. A higher power (fate, the life force,
    God) has put them together. Lovers feel out of control.
    Tom and Alice's love, especially sexual desire, seemed
    to be involuntary and out of their conscious control. It
    was as if they couldn't stop having sex or touching each
    other. When separated, each partner experienced intrusive
    thoughts about their beloved that often disrupted what-
    ever they were doing.

SPECIAL, UNIQUE, AND EXCLUSIVE: The lovers' fated destiny makes their relationship exclusive and special. Lovers talk about their partner's physical attributes (the dimple in his chin, the sound of her voice, his smell, his tall handsomeness).

SPONTANEITY: Everything with the lover gradually becomes easier. Talking is easier for both partners. Both partners let down their defenses. When in-love, the conversation between the lovers is spontaneous and relaxed. A statement I heard over and over again was, "I've never been able to talk to anyone like I do with _____."

AMAZING SEX: The sex life becomes more and more spontaneous and uninhibited. Lovers in-love create a spontaneous sex life without boundaries. They throw all restraint to the wind. If they marry, this behavior will end. As their marriage progresses, they will gradually stop and move into a nurturing kind of behavior once each partner has developed a solid sense of self, instead of engaging in the "let it all hang out," almost animal-like sex. I'm in no way putting down having "nurturing lovemaking"; it's the ideal, and some couples have it throughout their marriage. Alice and Tom felt safe enough to let their imaginations run wild, and sex became a form of play for each of them. They actually did things with each other that they had only fantasized about before.

SHARING SHAME SECRETS: Tom and Alice told each other things they had never shared with anyone else. For instance, Tom had cheated one of his partners out of his share of a financial gain. Alice told Tom some bizarre fantasies she'd had while masturbating, and expressed her fear that she was perverted. Tom worried about the size of his penis; something he shared with Alice for the first time (although every man I counseled with worried about his penis size). Alice shared her worries about her flat chest.

EXAGGERATED NEW ENERGY AND VITALITY: Alice and Tom made love for hours at a time. They needed far less sleep than usual. They talked on the phone for hours at a time. They dropped everything and took plane trips just to have sex with each other.

POSITIVITY: Lovers transform each other's shortcomings into strengths. One woman told me, "I just love Harry; he is so honest, he told me he killed a man. It was only our third date." I know he had good reasons for the killing, and he shared his deepest secret with me!" In-love partners see flaws in each other but have an exaggerated ability to reframe and to turn their partner's deficits into something positive.

MATE GUARDING: Because of their intense vulnerability, each partner is intensely jealous of any sign of interest their partner shows for the opposite sex. Each in-love partner is highly sensitive to any show of attention their partner had to a person of the same sex. Alice went into a tirade when Tom commented about Elizabeth Taylor's beauty.

ACHIEVE PERSONAL CHANGES: Alice was a jogger and worked out every day. Tom occasionally joined her whenever possible and almost effortlessly lost sixty pounds.

EXTREMELY VULNERABLE AND DEPENDENT ON PARTNER'S FEELINGS AND BEHAVIORS: In-love partners often change whatever they are doing to accommodate the other's slightest need or want. Tom canceled an important meeting in order to fly to Minnesota. A casual remark Tom made triggered Alice into having a liposuction procedure on her upper legs. Lover's desires seem to be identical, and their differences are trivialized. Each partner has tremendous emotional energy and passion for the other and feels utterly dependent on each other. Each is highly sensitive to the other's words and facial expressions. Each experiences dramatic mood swings triggered by their fantasy about their partner's feelings and behaviors.

Tom was caught in a spell of Mother Nature's old black magic. He was drunk in an addictive attachment and literally out of his mind. He was infatuated with Alice. Infatuation is a word that means "lacking sound judgment." It also means being carried away by shallow love and affection.

Alice was less smitten; she wanted a rich husband to take care of her and her children and to move to a warm climate. After a year and five months, when it was clear to Alice that Tom was not going to marry her, she had another lover within a week. Tom suffered gut-wrenching pain when she broke off the relationship. He was surprised that he could feel such physical suffering over the loss, but if you understand that romantic love is a trancelike, altered state of consciousness, you can compare Tom to a heroin addict whose fix has been abruptly taken from him. Being in-love is certainly deeper and richer than being a heroin addict, but the analogy helps explain why the withdrawal is so agonizing.

You may not be able to identify with all of these behaviors (some of you probably can add some of your own). The core element of this in-love stage (which we'll be referring to as the "romance program") is the feeling of ownership and possession. Lovers in-love believe their partners have been given to them, and that each is the other's destiny. This is the core of Post-Romantic Stress Disorder in all its levels of intensity.

3

The "New Discoveries" About Timeless Issues: Being In-Love, Lust, and Attachment

*Our results changed my thinking about the
very essence of Romantic love. I came to see this passion
as a fundamental human drive . . . it is a physiological
need, a profound urge, an instinct to court and
win a particular mating partner.*

—Helen Fisher, *Why We Love*

Tom and Alice's romance story shows us Mother Nature's old black magic at work. While their in-love sexual behavior was not exactly typical (Alice's not wanting to engage in being sexually penetrated—but wanting to wildly engage in oral and anal sex, and randomly cheating on her own rules prohibiting intercourse), Tom and Alice's behavior does show us the immense power and extraordinary passion that being in-love brings with it. Tom was completely smitten and suffered greatly when Alice left him. Alice was sexually smitten but the exclusivity and specialness (he's the one and no other) were diluted by her need to get married. Her telling Tom that a wealthy man in her church had bought her a house and a car and was giving her money every month should've given him pause and/or driven him away. The old man (the church "sugar daddy") was urging Alice to get married. This explained her urgency and her need to marry. Still, the "story" of Tom and Alice shows how unexpected and unpredictable falling in-love can be and how the in-love experience very often transcends both partner's plans and expectations. The in-love experience, as I've stated in Chapter 2, is a bona fide "altered state of consciousness."

BULLDOG:
AN EXPATRIATE IN THE LAND OF IN-LOVE

I have an acquaintance, nicknamed Bulldog (a fictitious nickname to protect his privacy), an admitted in-love addict, who went to Spain on a vacation. While there, he fell in-love with a lady named Isabella. He was so smitten, he married her and never returned to the United States. In the one conversation I've had with him, he sounded like a broken record, saying, "I can't believe I'm married to someone as young and beautiful as Isabella and that I wound up living in Spain." Bulldog is seventy-three years old; Isabella is thirty-eight. His original plan was to live on his ninety-year-old mother's farm in Oklahoma, but the best-laid plans are sidetracked by Mother Nature's old black magic!

THREE BRAIN PROGRAMS: A BLUEPRINT FOR OUR FUTURE

Helen Fisher has presented some compelling research, asserting that each of us is endowed by nature with three unique, innate brain programs: an "in-love" or romance program, a "lust" program, and an "attachment" program. Fisher's book *Why We Love: The Nature and Chemistry of Romantic Love* is a *must* read. It will give you a rich background for my ideas about Post-Romantic Stress Disorder. I take full responsibility for my interpretation of her research.

These three newly discovered unique brain programs offer us evolutionary benefits. In order for our unrepeatable DNA and bloodline to continue, we must produce offspring. In order to do that, we have to find a desirable mate and have a child. The three brain programs guide us in our "meeting, mating, and procreating," as Dr. Pat Love puts it. Meeting, mating, and procreating are the way the "life force" manifests itself to ensure that our bloodline and DNA are carried on. Love's book *The Truth About Love: The Highs, the Lows, and How You Can*

Make It Last Forever is another *must* read. It offers some rich guidelines that aid all of us in resolving the issues spawned by post-romantic stress disorder.

OUR NEED TO LOVE

Recently, I became very moved when I watched the television special celebrating the Beatles' fiftieth anniversary of their first appearance on *The Ed Sullivan Show*, the famous variety show that was must-see television back in the day. Hearing their music this night was a different experience for me. While I know nothing of the inner dynamics of their music, or exactly what constitutes rock and roll, I heard archetypical themes at the heart of their songs.

ARCHETYPES

I ended my book *Homecoming* with a line from Steven Spielberg's brilliant movie *E.T. the Extra-Terrestrial*. When E.T. longingly looks at Elliot and says, "Home Elliot, home," people of all colors, races, and religions felt a chill of recognition run down their spines. It was because that one line had touched our "collective unconscious" where the longing for peace, security, connectedness (home) is there in all of us—the one line touched the archetype of our spiritual longing.

Lines from the Beatles' song "Hey Jude" express the universal longing in everyone's heart to find our special mate, one we can settle down with and with whom we can make a family. Whether we like it or not, we long for a partner to reveal ourselves to, to be intimate with, and to partner with to produce offspring. This longing takes form when we fall in-love or as we say in our nontechnical speech, "When Cupid's arrow hits us."

THE ROMANCE PROGRAM

So-called primitive people echo an understanding of love's dynamic process. In *Why We Love*, Fisher quotes Taita of Kenya (p. 87), who said that love comes in two forms: one is "an irresistible longing, a kind of sickness." The other is a "deep, enduring affection for each other." These sum up the three brain programs—when we "fall in-love," we *fall*! We can't stop thinking about our beloved. They are "special," and we want to be with them and them alone. Our whole personalities change; the penny-pincher starts lavishing gifts on his beloved; the woman who hardly liked to be touched is now a roaring volcano of sexual desire. Both partners' testosterone (the chemical that is the energy behind the sex drive) goes up considerably. I counseled both high-T (high-testosterone) and low-T men and women who were in-love. They were either totally out of their normal physical sexual comfort zone or thought they had died and were in heaven while in-love. The sexual highs are the result of the chemicals that are released when we fall in-love. The PEA dopamine cocktail that I discussed in Chapter 2 had been studied but remained a hypothesis prior to Fisher's work.

Fisher and her colleagues found that powerful chemicals rooted in the caudate nucleus—a part of the brain's reward system—triggers dopamine, probably norepinephrine, and decreases serotonin, which seem to be the chemicals that trigger the ecstatic elements that compromise the romance program. This is why rejected lovers feel so angry. They are losing something—the amazing sex—that is incredibly rewarding and pleasurable, as well as the comfort and spontaneity they had while being in-love.

Previous research has shown that the feeling of "falling in-love" is produced by specific chemicals and networks in the brain. Fisher believes that falling in-love, or what she calls the romance program, is innate and a fundamental human drive, much like craving food and water. She even likens it to the maternal instinct. She concludes that the drive to fall in-love "is a physiological need, a profound urge, an instinct to court and win a particular mating partner" (*Why We Love,* p. xv). Fisher and her team found that "lust" and "attachment" were also separate innate brain programs. Romance (being in-love), lust, and attachment are governed by three distinct areas of the brain, and each is driven by its own unique goal.

Over a period of six years, Fisher and her colleagues scanned the brains of more than 140 men and women who were madly in-love. Half of the samples were men and women whose love was reciprocated, while the rest had been rejected by the person they were in-love with. Fisher and her colleagues used a new form of brain scanning known as functional magnetic resonance imaging (fMRI). The fMRI measured the blood flow activity in specific brain regions. Scientists already knew which kind of nerves connect with which kinds of brain regions (*Why We Love,* pp. 69–70). Fisher also constructed a fifty-five-part questionnaire on the feeling of being in-love (being infatuated or being strongly romantically attracted to someone). She also questioned a sample of lovers who had been rejected. The results of her research were startling in several aspects. They validated her belief in the innate romance program and the powerful chemicals that are the source of it.

THE LENGTH OF
THE ROMANCE PROGRAM

Fisher's research found that the romance program lasts for about seventeen months. Our couple from Chapter 2, Alice and Tom, bear out this finding. Alice left Tom seventeen months after their romance started. Other research has found that the duration of the "in-love" program is twelve to eighteen months. When it ends, the wild ecstasy (amazing sex), obsessive thoughts about one's lover, the need to be together, and other elements of being in-love, such as the need to talk for hours on the phone and constantly kiss and touch each other, diminished slowly and left lovers in the state I'm calling Post-Romantic Stress Disorder.

PARADISE LOST

As the chemistry of being in-love diminishes during the romance program, the high level of testosterone that is triggered by the passion of being in-love also diminishes. Each partner's sex drive goes back to where it was before they fell in-love. However, often the lovers—one or both—mistake this natural and necessary equilibrium as a sign that they've fallen out of love. Many of the partners will ride out this leveling-out phase, stay attached, and do the work necessary to make their love deep and enduring. However, those who confuse being "in-love" with mature love often end the relationship or stay in a relationship characterized by childish conflicts, resentment, and anger.

THE END AS THE BEGINNING

The worst-case scenario when people leave the in-love phase is that one of the lovers moves into one of the most extreme forms of PRSD, which involves violence to self, the partner, or sometimes to both. Fisher's work, as well as that of others, makes it clear that the end of the romance program is simply the first phase of building a solid sense of personalized adult love for both partners. This "work" of love can be the most exciting part of the love two people begin to create with each other. Nature wants complexity, not strict compatibility. Spousal differences over family of origin rules, conflicts, and the clash of wounded selfhood mark Stage 1 of love-building, and often becomes the first degree of PRSD.

IS FALLING IN-LOVE
A CHANCE HAPPENING?

Contrary to popular belief, Fisher and her team showed that there is nothing accidental or capricious about falling in-love. We now know that we are born fully equipped for romance, just waiting for the exact moment when we will meet the right partner who will ignite our romance program. We rarely fall in-love at first sight, although it certainly can happen. But it usually doesn't take long to trigger one or both of the soon-to-be-lover's primordial brain networks, eagerly waiting for mating, sexual ecstasy, and reproduction.

The lust program most often follows the romance program, because of the neurotransmitter dopamine releasing testosterone, the hormone of sexual desire. The injection of dopamine in a male's blood system immediately stimulates the desire for copulatory behaviors. Base levels of testosterone are inherited. In layman's terms, some people are "hornier" than others.

The romance program is extremely powerful because it must ensure that our evolutionary genes are passed on. When one partner realizes that the other's sexual desire has waned, they often move to end the relationship, most often with a perfectly decent and adequate partner. This is the major tragedy of PRSD.

To sum up, our three innate programs ensure that the species will continue. Falling in-love (romance) most often triggers lust (sexual desire), and as a couple engages in months of amazing sex, they become compassionately attached (the attachment program) and desire to make a home in preparation for having children. The dopamine and norepinephrine are partly replaced by vasopressin and oxytocin and the serotonin returns to normal.

THE LUST PROGRAM

People can intuitively distinguish the feeling of romance (being in-love) and that of lust. You can have sex with another person without wanting to marry them. People can also distinguish between the feeling of romance and attachment. Once attached, the intense state of being in-love subsides and with it the elevated and ecstatic sexual drive. Romantic love most often triggers the lust program; it certainly did for Tom and Alice. But does lust always stimulate romantic love? Can a woman climb in bed with a male friend at work, or even a stranger, and fall in-love with him?

It can happen, but it is not the usual way that falling in-love happens. As Fisher says, "Lust does not necessarily lead to the passion and obsession of romantic love. The brain circuitry of lust does not necessarily ignite the furnace of Romance" (*Why We Love*, p. 85).

Casual Sex

But Mother Nature's old black magic is quite fickle. The chemistry of sexual desire and copulation can trigger the fuel of romance. This is why it can be really dangerous to have sex with someone you know you don't wish to have a long-term involvement with. So-called casual sex is far more dangerous than people think. You may intend to only have casual sex and wind up falling in-love.

"The Oldest Lion of Them All"

An Italian proverb calls lust "the oldest lion of them all." Lust is a primordial brain program that, from an evolutionary point of view, ensures the continuance of the human race; lust was there before the "romance" and "attachment" programs—it had to be. Without it, humans would have become extinct long ago. We need to be able to lust in order to continue human life as we know it. A minority of people confuse being in-love with lust. The majority of people in diverse cultures know that lust is different from being in-love. The in-love program evolved when lust was already there. Lust is the universal drive (feeling) to have sex with a person who turns you on. You can feel lust almost any place and at any time.

The purpose of lust is simply to have sex with someone. Lust wants sexual release and it is *only* about sexual release. This urge is different from the feeling of romantic love. Romantic love often triggers lust, and lust can trigger romantic love.

Jonas: An In-Love Addict

One of my counseling clients, a seventy-four-year-old man I'll call "Jonas," often complained to me that neither one of his two ex-wives fit the image of the women he lusted for. Jonas was attracted to dark-haired, large-breasted women with large, fleshy buttocks and an unshaven pubic region. I asked him if he would have any of the women he lusted after as a wife and the mother of his children. "Oh, God no!" he told me, emphatically. He said that since his last divorce (from his second wife), he had a number of trysts with women who fit his lust image. "The last thing I wanted was to settle down with them. They were for sex alone. They were *dirty legs*." This term, used frequently during my own teenage years, was a gross appellation for raunchy, promiscuous women. Jonas was an in-love addict. He had extramarital affairs during both his marriages. He had children but hardly spent any time with them. His attachment program lacked nurturing. He was a biological father but nothing more—basically just a sperm donor.

"Let the World Go Away"

Once in-love you want alone time with your "special one." As the song says, the world goes away, and you don't care as long as you are with your newly discovered soul mate. Lovers ensconced in their romance program lose temporary interest in pretty much everything that they found motivating and exciting prior to falling in-love. After the in-love hangover subsides, they will renew those interests. For people who are operating out of lust, it is "slam bam, thank you, ma'am," or my made-up women's version, "huddle, cuddle, but don't pop my bubble." The lust partner wants to go home in the morning (sometimes right after orgasm). The raw joke about coyote sex is a good illustration of lust. As the joke goes, the lusting partner reaches climax and wants to leave. But the object of his lust cuddles up to him. So he bites his own arm off to get out of there! This is coyote sex. While I've used a male example, this could apply to either men or women.

Lust Seeks Control

Being in-love feels like you are "out of control." When you lust, you're calculating and cunning. Lust involves some planning and control. People everywhere have used what they hoped was an aphrodisiac to trigger lust.

Tomatoes (love apples) were often placed in brothels. Other supposed aphrodisiacs are shark fins, oysters, lobsters, hyena eyes, powdered rhino horns, goose tongues, chocolate, caviar, pomegranates, beer, dates, figs, prunes, and pulverized beetle, aka "Spanish fly," to mention but a few. These things have been used for centuries at different times and in various cultures to turn each other on sexually. I can remember well the day my buddy Joe offered me a hit of Spanish fly. I was sixteen and already "hornier than a rabbit in heat." I gulped it down with water and waited. For more than a week, nothing happened, and I was crushed. I hoped for exotic dreams and loads of ammunition to masturbate with. At that age, I had already engaged in sex with several prostitutes in the then wide-open brothels in Galveston, Texas. My hope of an extraordinary evening with the "ladies of the night" dissolved like the Spanish fly pills I swallowed. The lust program operates independently of the romance program, as well as the attachment program. This means we can love someone and be securely attached to them and still lust after another.

THE ATTACHMENT PROGRAM

After the twelve- to eighteen-month duration of being in-love, our energy and passion begin to wane. Either before or after a child has been conceived, a new program starts to kick in. Sometime before the disappointment over the end of the wild sexual ecstasy, couples have more than likely begun to experience each other in a new way. The in-love madness has succumbed to new feelings of security, comfort, and union with your lover. From an evolutionary perspective, nature provides this attachment program so that there will be parental partners there to nurture and care for offspring. Parents need a new brain program in order to seal their togetherness and to move them to want to have and care for their offspring. This new feeling is considered by many to be a mirror of the attachment program that you had with your mothering source. A "good enough" attachment bond has been called your "secure base," and everyone needs such a foundation. According to psychologist Elaine Hatfield, the attachment program allows you to reignite the empathetic reunion you had in your earliest symbiotic bonding. Ideally, spouses become each other's secure base.

The problem is that many people are not securely attached in infancy. They range from being "avoidantly" attached, to being "ambivalently attached" to a small group who are "disoriently attached." In my book *Reclaiming Virtue* (pp. 112–15), I describe what is called the "infant strange" situation, which was an experiment designed by Mary Ainsworth, and later Mary Main, to measure the kind of attachment an infant and her mother (or a mothering source) have established. (We will further discuss attachment deficits and how to heal them in Chapter 8.) Fisher describes attachment as a "feeling of happy togetherness with someone whose life has become deeply entwined with yours."

The attachment program is the foundation that we will build on in Part II, when we tackle the "work of love." The feeling of attachment is less intense, energetic, and obsessive than the feeling of romantic love and lust.

Couples inevitably move from being in-love and lusting after their partner to enhancing their attachment. At that point, they have definitely "fallen out of love." The new discoveries make it clear that being in-love is the nonworking prelude to the other stages of building a rich friendship and deepened intimacy, along with a satisfactory sex life. True love is a process. It takes time and work to create mature love. With and without these "new discoveries" of the three innate brain programs, lovers realize that the in-love chemical bath (the brain sprinkled with dopamine and norepinephrine, reduced serotonin, and releasing lots of testosterone) has to subside. No one can have a normal life sustaining the in-love intensity of the romance program.

For those who are co-dependent and carrying attachment issues rooted in abandonment, abuse (physical, sexual, emotional, and/or spiritual), special trauma, and/or parental enmeshment issues, the condition that I'm calling post-romantic stress disorder in one of its degrees of intensity is quite likely to happen to you (we'll be looking at PRSD in detail in Chapter 4).

The new discoveries of these three innate brain programs give us an adult understanding about the enormous differences between being in-love and lust and the entrance into the third developmental stage of mature love, the attachment program. These brain programs make it clear that "romantic love did *not evolve to help us maintain a partnership*" (Fisher, *Why We Love*, p. 92; my emphasis). It evolved for different purposes: to help us meet someone we physically and emotionally desire, a "special" unique partner—the one person and no other, regardless of whether they measure up to an idealized "lust image" (which they almost never do). Mother Nature's old black magic is the answer to the haunting question: Why this one and not that one?

THE BIOLOGY OF MATE SELECTION

In Chapter 1 of my first love book, *Creating Love*, I wrote about the "bafflement of love." In a rather gross example, I spoke of one of my unofficial jobs as a checker at a popular neighborhood grocery store when I was fifteen. My checking station was at the front of the store. When a shapely woman came into the store, I was to push a buzzer that signaled Leon in the produce department, and Bubba and Phil in the meat department, alerting them that a good-looking female had entered the store. Over a period of time, it wasn't the gorgeous females we focused on so much but the nerdy guy she was with, or vice versa—the handsome man who had a less physically attractive wife. I vividly remember Leon stating through his two missing front teeth, "It's a goddamn shame there ain't more of *me* to go around!" as he spit out his wad of chewing tobacco. At that time, Leon was on his fourth marriage, and as I'm sure my description has rendered in your mind, he was certainly no catch! This wondering about mate selection has been a mystery down through the ages. How did he/she end up with *that* person?

DNA DIFFERENCES

Other contemporary research has aided our understanding of meeting and mating: why the romance trance causes us to choose this woman or man and not that one. Some clarification was given by early research on tissue rejection in organ transplants. Scientists found that the body can actually recognize familiar and unfamiliar DNA. Our bodies can, in fact, detect compatible as well as incompatible genes. In an article by Claus Wedekind entitled "MHC-Dependent Mate Preferences in Humans," which appeared in the *Proceedings of the Royal Society in London* (260:245–49), he and his team reported that the smell of a man's sweaty T-shirt was most desirable to a given woman when his human lymphocyte antigen (HLA) profile varied the most from her own. This means that women are attracted to the scent of men whose DNA is least like their own.

Here's what Dr. Pat Love writes about HLA:

> The DNA . . . functions as the immune system's disease detector. An individual HLA codes for a limited number of diseases and passes on this ability to potential offspring through DNA. However, if this individual mates with a person with a different HLA code, then their offspring will have immunity to far more diseases (The Truth About Love, pp. 31–32).

We feel chemistry when we find a person with a suitable DNA match (i.e., those whose DNA is compatible but is least like our own). You may think you know what you were attracted to in your mate, and hopefully your love has evolved. The theories of "love map" and imago are valuable to know. But in the beginning, it was Mother Nature's old black magic at work. She always wants increasing complexity.

The new discoveries about the science of love make it clear that all three unique brain programs are necessary to ensure the evolution of human life. Research has shown that when couples are open and willing to learn and work on enriching the attachment program, three well-observed, self-generating developmental stages emerge in the process of creating a rich, unique, and self-actualizing shared love.

In Part II, I will offer an open and flexible model (with experiential exercises) to guide you on the journey of creating your own style of mature love. There is no such thing as getting love right! Love requires two people whose flexible sense of *self* is evolving. (I'll discuss the creation of a flexible and solid sense of self in Chapter 11.) But there are commonalities in happily married couples that have been studied over the years. We can use these commonalities as our guidelines in Part II. But before we get there, let's turn to a more in-depth discussion of Post-Romantic Stress Disorder.

4

Post-Romantic Stress Disorder

WHO ORDERED, THAT THEIR LONGING'S FIRE
SHOULD BE, AS SOON AS KINDLED, COOLED?

—*Matthew Arnold*

In *The Truth About Love*, Dr. Pat Love courageously writes about what I'm calling Post-Romantic Stress Disorder (PRSD):

These convictions (lack of sexual desire) lead to an action that remains the deepest regret of my life, an unnecessary divorce from a thoroughly decent, loving man and the father of my two children. We believed we had fallen out of love.

PRSD is a root cause of many painful marriages and a multitude of unnecessary divorces. I've noticed this phenomenon for the last forty years. Modern anthropology, neuroscience, and brain research have provided scientific data that may help us understand it.

In my twenty years of counseling couples, I've seen roughly 150 people leave perfectly good marriages and/or relationships because of PRSD. The recently discovered research on the chemistry of the brain and how it affects us in all areas of our lives was not available to me in the early days of my counseling, but it was absolutely clear that most people who ended their relationships had a lot going for them. Still, one or the other's disorder of sexual desire spawned a mistaken belief that they had "fallen out of love." It was also clear that many of these divorcees had a very damaged sense of self.

In another place in her book *The Truth About Love*, Dr. Love writes, "the evidence is clear that without proper information and guidelines you can easily make serious mistakes" (p. 17). It is certainly a deadly serious mistake to end a perfectly or potentially good future marriage for reasons that are erroneous or misunderstood. The "1999 Rutgers National Marriage Project" reported that in one survey after another people put "a satisfactory love relationship" at the top of their desire for happiness list, yet our divorce rate today is higher than at any other time in modern history! In this project, the main reason people gave for not wanting to get married was fear of divorce, and they also feared that if they got married, they would wind up being dissatisfied and unhappy.

With a more than 50 percent divorce rate and only 33 percent of people saying they are happy in their union, people have good reasons to fear marriage. Many of the people I've talked to over the years told me of the large number of people they knew who felt trapped in dull, boring marriages, who were bonded by the "terror of aloneness," and who felt that there was something or someone better waiting around the corner—although they felt that they could not afford to venture out and look for them.

Many of my clients were enduring long, unhappy marriages. Many simply took their vows seriously, though they felt the sting of "quiet desperation." For some, divorce was too costly and impractical. Many stayed married for their children, even after the children had grown up. Many people stay married for religious reasons, and I know several people who have endured very unfulfilling marriages because their faith prohibits divorce. I have an acquaintance whose sixty-one-year marriage could be called anything but happy and fulfilling. His religious beliefs prohibit divorce, but I'm sure his faith is not the sole reason he stays married. His religion also prohibits infidelity, and he has had numerous affairs. I found that one or both partners in a majority of the long-term endurance marriages had had one or more affairs.

I believe that most of the long-term marriages had begun with good enough attachment programs. Later on, one or both partners said, "I love my spouse, but I'm not in-love with them" (the husband said this more often). They were referring to the warmth and the security of creating a home, and in the majority of cases, the shared experiences of bearing offspring. The ones who went on and were docile enough to seek help, worked on their unresolved childhood issues, and learned new skills—especially conflict resolution skills—and achieved a plateau kind of intimacy that sometimes had nearly the ecstasy of being in-love. The ones who did nothing and stayed in marriages that I describe as bonded by the "terrors of aloneness" were still hampered by the sexual issues caused by the cessation of the wild, amazing sex and by the "differences" between their self and their partner. They were also conflicted by their own "wounds" from the past and a "fractured sense of self."

TOM AND ALICE: AFTER THE FALL

When Tom and Alice broke up, Tom was devastated. He started binge drinking and became almost suicidal. I counseled him for a long time after Alice left him. It took three months before he let go of the fantasy that Alice would come back to him. At times he felt physical, gut-wrenching pain, and at other times he felt a knot in his throat that almost stopped him from speaking. This last symptom is a good description of the shame he felt because Alice had left him. Intense feelings of shame are accompanied by the inability to "speak." He slowly began dating after a nine-month hiatus and was gradually restored to a high degree of normalcy. During the last two months of their courtship, Alice began secretly dating another man. Tom discovered this two weeks before she ended the relationship.

He was so panicked by the discovery that he frantically tried to restore their "love," but to no avail. Within a year, the new lover, who was quite wealthy according to what Alice's best friend told Tom, married her.

Alice could easily be described as a "sex and in-love addict." She once told me that she had gone through nine lovers in a two-year period before she met Tom. Tom learned from a mutual friend that Alice had had an affair during the second year of her new marriage. Alice avoided PRSD by immediately remarrying, and when the sex diminished, she started a new affair. This pattern will likely go on and on until she gets some help.

In the last ten years, there has been more sound information on romance, mate selection, marriage, attachment, and family health than at any other time in our history. In my book *Bradshaw On: The Family*, I shared the family systems theory of emotional disease. In this book, I'm sharing the new discoveries about being in-love, lust, and attachment, and the strong and flexible sense of self needed in long-term relationships. We are examining the ecstasy and the agony of PRSD.

SANDRA AND COLBY:
A CASE OF MADONNA ANOREXIA

Sandra was a high-T woman. She was devastated when a sexual breach happened with her fiancé, Colby. Sandra and Colby were in the British Virgin Islands for a week's vacation. One afternoon Sandra decided to dress up in a sexy nurse's outfit in order to have a new sexual experience with Colby. When Sandra came out of the bathroom in her sexy garb, Colby completely shut down. Later, in our therapy session, Colby said he liked her outfit but he suddenly felt his body tense up and was hardly able to breathe. This had happened to him frequently in his first marriage. He had what I've come to call "Madonna anorexia (MA)." The message in his head said, "You don't have sex with someone you love and cherish" and certainly you can't "fuck" with them. Colby's rejection was shaming and disrupted what had been an "I-thou in-love" relationship.

Sandra told me in a counseling session that she would never initiate sex again. In later counseling sessions with both of them, I noticed that when anything related to sex came up, she reexperienced feelings related to the initial PRSD and withdrew from the conversation. The first sexual breach was powerful enough to color every other aspect of their marriage. (I use the word *breach* to describe the first jolt of PRSD.) I'm using the word breach in the way Dr. Jay Wagener, an excellent psychiatrist in Los Angeles, uses it in his soon to be published book, *The Breach*. Dr. Wagener describes a breach (which can happen in every aspect of our relational lives) by saying, "Where there was once a 'we,' now there is an 'I.'" Your conscious and unconscious beliefs and expectations about a person you care about are ruptured and you feel a loss and feel alone.

Sandra punished Colby in subtle ways over the next five years. He ultimately filed for a divorce in the midst of her shock, anger, and chagrin. Although Madonna anorexia seems to be primarily a male phenomenon, it is traumatic for both partners. For the partner being rejected, the breach can be devastating!

BILL AND SUE: DRIVEN TO PRSD

I counseled another couple I'll call Bill and Sue, who claimed to be madly and wildly in-love. Bill was ten years younger than Sue. They went through almost all the behaviors I enumerated throughout Chapter 2. After two years, they married. This is when I observed what I'd seen before. Initially, I saw all the elements of Post-Traumatic Stress Disorder (PTSD). Much work has been done on PTSD in recent years. Two of my senior fellow colleagues at The Meadows treatment center in Wickenburg, Arizona—Dr. Bessel van der Kolk and Dr. Steven Levine—have both done pioneering, breakthrough research on PTSD, and Drs. Shelley Ulram, Claudia Black, and Pat Carnes have developed their own approaches to reducing the pain of PTSD. It is now understood that having just one catastrophic experience while you are powerless is enough to cause the disorder (regardless if we're talking about war, abuse, or relationships).

The cessation of the amazing sex experienced during the romance program is often very traumatic for both partners. When asked if something is wrong and the lover experiencing the "sexual breach" responds that everything is "fine," it is often an expression of anger due to the withdrawal of intense pleasure. If the rejected partner's anger is not dealt with, it will come out in passive-aggressive behaviors toward the low-T partner. These behaviors, intended as punishments, may be just thoughtless (such as consistently showing up late for meals that the partner has spent a long time preparing, or refusing to eat a beautifully prepared meal) or purposefully mean-spirited (such as destroying an object that the partner loves, losing a partner's jewelry, or stealing an heirloom). Regardless of the degree of hurt, these behaviors can cut deeply to the core and can be emotionally and/or physically destructive.

PTSD is characterized by a painful experience (a scene) becoming entrenched in the amygdala, the part of the brain concerned with emotion and motivation. The expression of the shock resulting from the trauma is locked into the body just as the emotional expression is frozen in the past. When a similar aspect of the past trauma is perceived, it triggers the original traumatic experience. (In Chapter 8, we will learn how to heal this trauma with natural resources.)

Post-Romantic Stress Disorder, PRSD, emerges in marriages when the romance gene diminishes and the amazing sex stage comes to an end. PRSD is often the offspring of PTSD. Early in their marriage, Bill and Sue had a childish quarrel related to Sue's driving ability. She was not the best driver, which in their early courtship years Bill found endearing and "cute." As their relationship progressed, however, he had grown weary of Sue's general driving habits, though he had tolerated them and usually kept his mouth shut. One day, Sue was driving Bill's car and scraped the fender by sideswiping a curb. A near miss was one thing, but the physical damage to his car sent Bill over the edge. He raged at her—a behavior Sue had never seen before. The quarrel over Sue's driving diluted the intensity of the PEA/dopamine (the love molecule), which had persisted far beyond eighteen months for them. Rage is not characteristic during the romance period.

Several events slowly followed the night of the quarrel, actions that snowballed and eventually turned into an avalanche of ill will. First, Sue refused to be sexual for the first time. The rage-filled rant Bill had engaged in hurt her and made her feel angry, and making love to him was the last thing she wanted to do. Bill felt angry and hurt by this, not connecting the dots between his behavior and her reaction, and withdrew to the guest bedroom to be alone. Sue had a very low testosterone level; Bill's libido was much higher. Extensive PRSD generally does not happen all at once, but an initial sexual breach, such as the one between Bill and Sue, can slowly and surely create a certain discrepancy of sexual desire between partners that can become the status quo. Many marriage therapists believe that "discrepancy of sexual desire" is the number one problem in marital conflict. If not worked out, many couples ultimately divorce over this issue—a tragic outcome! My guess is that we would reduce the divorce rate to 15 percent if couples would stop leaving their perfectly good enough marital partners.

Besides withholding sex, the quarrel Bill and Sue had over the scratched fender triggered a number of other behaviors that made it fairly clear that the infatuation stage was over. Bill started playing golf on both weekend days. During the intense period of their courtship, Bill had kept Sunday open as "their" special day. Sue resumed her social life with her best friends, which involved a Wednesday girls' night out. She had left the group during her courtship with Bill.

As their marriage progressed, Bill and Sue infrequently had the amazing sex that being in-love had provided them in the early stages of their relationship. The quarrel was a benchmark that changed their sex life, but their life together didn't end. Many of the magical in-love aspects of the initial stages had slowly faded away. After the love cocktail wore off, Bill told me that their conversations seemed more controlled, less spontaneous and easy. When they did have sex, they noticed that it was harder to become fully aroused, and at times they felt some vague disappointment afterward. Other things changed, too. Each partner felt more constricted and had a need for more space, and felt the desire for more spontaneity in their relationship. While they were in the romantic trance, both Bill and Sue had often rearranged their work schedules, often calling in sick in order to spend the day together. Realistically, think of how little you would get done if that wild, passionate, amazing sex never went away!

As the infatuation phase diminishes, each person must resume their former life. This is healthy and normal. All couples had work, friends, and rituals they neglected during the in-love stage. Once married, spouses both want and need to renew their established friendships. Sometimes this can be easily done, while other times it can be quite difficult. One partner may have a friendship with another person who's married. The new husband may not like the husband of his wife's best friend—this is often difficult to work out.

Neither Bill nor Sue had dealt with each other's family of origin rules, both overt and covert, during their courtship phase. They hadn't worked on the traumas they each had from childhood, nor did they even understand their unresolved developmental dependency need deficits (DDDs). Fortunately, Bill and Sue actually did the work, which I'll describe in Part II, and worked out a good enough, satisfying sex life. Twenty years later, they have achieved a deep love that sustains them.

The overarching issue that I dealt with in counseling most couples was the discrepancy of sexual drive. There is such intensity in the amazing sex stage during the romance program. People with very low levels of testosterone are amazed at how sexual they become. I've often counseled women who said that they never thought they could have the sex drive they have with their partners. People who formerly had little desire to be touched want to be held, touched, and cuddled a lot of the time. When all of these intense desires end, it is baffling to both partners. After months of unusual and amazing sex, it's very easy to think you don't love this person anymore when the "sexual passion" diminishes.

As we saw in Chapters 1 and 2, our culture (through love stories, myths, and movies) stresses that sexual desire equals love. This belief is blatantly untrue. The in-love program ends in twelve to eighteen months, and then partners return to their pre-romance testosterone levels. I've had many married male and female clients say they are still in-love with a former courtship partner. This is often because that partner ended their relationship. Or, in certain clients, they had to leave the lover because the romance was going nowhere. These clients were ready to get married and wanted children.

The point here is that a courtship partner may still feel the hormonal power of the PEA/dopamine cocktail, while some healthy and informed partners work to keep the sexual fires burning. Emotionally disturbed partners keep it going by stalking or abusing their ex-spouses or ex-girlfriends. If people have achieved a strong degree of attachment and ego strength, they go on, but slowly their past anger and resentment, as well as their unresolved dependency needs, begin to eat away at the soul of their relationship.

If they do not get some help, they unhappily endure the relationship, distract themselves, or triangulate with a person or activity. To triangulate means to turn your interest to another person or activity that eases the unresolved conflict with your spouse. For instance, a parent might throw herself wholeheartedly into her children's lives and activities to the detriment of her spousal relationship. Or perhaps she spends more and more time at the office, making work her de facto spouse. A husband might spend the majority of his free time on the weekend playing golf, as Bill did, or engaging in a hobby. Others might throw themselves into church and church-related activities. A partner might start drinking heavily, engage in self-sex, or begin an extramarital affair. Affairs—especially long-term ones—retrigger the romance program, making the affair seem like real "love," but often it's a sign of stunted growth and the inability to get beyond one's own baggage from the past (especially in terms of the DDDs, which we'll be exploring more fully in Chapter 8). If a couple does stay together but doesn't work toward enriching their marriage and building a strong sense of self, their relationship often slowly degenerates into two people living like bunk buddies bonded by the "terrors of aloneness."

After years of being involved in counseling and studying psychological matters, I believe PRSD is the risky shadow of fulfilling love. In Chapter 5, I'll talk about the malevolent offspring of PRSD in its darkest roles—stalking, battering, "love suicide," domestic murder, emotional heartache, and rejected love, a distress that in my opinion is often only second in its emotional impact to death itself. In fact, some find death more desirable and either kill themselves, their spouse, or both.

PRSD: IN-LOVE HANGOVER

As said earlier, the enchantment of the in-love/romance brain program diminishes after about twelve to eighteen months into a relationship. Put into layman's terms, infatuation is like a potent martini, and PRSD is the inevitable hangover. It's the contrast between heightened feelings of pleasure and invincibility to those of pain and nausea. To go from the emotional penthouse to the cellar—seemingly overnight—can be extremely traumatic. Addicts urgently try to find their drug of choice as soon as they can in an attempt to feel good again. They want the high-T that came with the in-love amazing sex.

Some of the high-T love partners who stay with their beloved secretly masturbate with pornography or get hooked on cybersex. Many were sex and love addicts when they fell in-love. When their in-love flounders, they move back to their sex addiction, which may include phone sex, massage parlors, affairs, or cybersex. Sex and love addiction are most clearly recognized by multiple affairs.

SARAH AND JUDA: SELF-SEX SABOTAGE

A couple I counseled had been married for six years. They were coasting along with no public signs of dysfunction. But Juda had a strong need for sex. Conversely, Sarah, a very low-T woman, had almost no desire for sex. Juda kept telling me how great their sexual relations had been when they were courting.

Sarah's presenting problem was that Juda was an Internet addict. Sarah described him as being online every moment he had available. She was curious to know what he was doing all those hours, so she checked and discovered that he had registered personal profiles on diverse dating sites. When confronted, Juda fluffed it off as a way he was dealing with being depressed. "It's all make-believe," he told Sarah. Sarah didn't believe that and confessed that their marriage was in a tailspin after this; her discovery made her lose trust in her husband. She further told me, "I'm no longer attracted to Juda, and I no longer feel attractive to him." This last remark seems to point to something that happens frequently when the partner is involved with addictive self-sex. When the spouse (usually the husband) is holed up and using self-sex to solve his PRSD problems, the wife feels less and less attractive. The husband never wants to have sex with her, not even "special occasions" like birthdays, Valentine's Day, or their wedding anniversary! This is a terrible blow to the spouse's self-esteem.

Sadly, Sarah and Juda's marriage never recovered. She filed for divorce one year after they came to me for counseling. Here again was a "good enough" marriage that could have been salvaged, if only they had cooperated in counseling. Their three children, all under six years old, had to pay the price for it. I made that very clear to them.

At one time in our lives, we've probably all been rejected by someone we were in-love with. It's painful and may even make you doubt yourself and your sense of worth. I've been through it once—and that's all the experiential knowledge I ever want.

Fisher's research has outlined the powerful chemicals that help us grasp the degree of dysfunction that PRSD can lead to. We will look at the most damaging behaviors in Chapter 5.

THE FOUR DEGREES OF PRSD

Post-Romantic Stress Disorder covers several behaviors and has degrees of intensity. For many, the first breaking off of the amazing sex experienced during the in-love stage of the relationship spreads over their marriage and creates a second degree of PRSD (severe bickering and unending conflicts), which leads to the third degree. The fourth is a result of unrequited love (divorce or just ending an in-love relationship). I put it as the fourth degree because it involves violence. The violation of emotional boundaries in stalking, or the abusing or killing the rejecting spouse, or killing oneself. Let's explore these stages in more detail.

First Degree of PRSD

The first degree covers the sense of shame that is experienced when an in-love trance is broken by diminished sexual desire in one partner. The first degree also covers the painful feeling of *rejection* when one partner wants to end the relationship or asks for a divorce.

Second Degree of PRSD

When partners who've experienced the sexual breach go on to marry and do nothing to deepen their attachment program, their marriage can degenerate and be dominated by the "no-listen, no-talk, and no-feel" unconscious rules. Conflict resolution degenerates into judgmental shaming, which triggers constant defensiveness, and creates distance and "dissmell," which I will elaborate on in Chapters 6 and 9. Both partners may keep up the facade of a spontaneous marriage, but when they get home, they avoid intimacy by withdrawal, or they create separation by arguing, raging, childish pouting, and other childish behavior. Their sex life usually deteriorates, and they are sexless for long periods of time. Both partners have failed to use the marital relationship as a resource for developing a solid sense of self.

Third Degree of PRSD

The partners slowly withdraw from each other, rarely having any real contact or connection. They often become sexual with themselves, chronically masturbating, with or without pornography (magazines, Internet, cybersex). Either partner (but usually the male) may become sexually addicted, extending his sexual behavior to partners on the Internet, or with phone sex, or going to "massage" parlors. They may have multiple affairs.

As one spouse becomes sexually addicted, the other spouse becomes a co-sex addict. He or she may also have an affair. This stage is characterized by a boring, unhappy marriage with long, long gaps between having sex (as Alan describes on the TV series *Two and a Half Men*—birthdays, anniversaries, and maybe Christmas). A perfect example of a more benign form of Stage 3 of PRSD is presented in the movie *Hope Springs*. Arnold (played by Tommy Lee Jones) and Kay (played by Meryl Streep) come to therapy after having been sexless for five years and living like roommates. (I will comment fully on the movie in the introduction to Part II of this book.) For some of my own clients, abstinence had been much longer!

Fourth Degree of PRSD

The fourth degree of PRSD involves the rejected spouse/lover. They remain in the throes of the romance program and refuse to accept that their marriage or love affair is over. This leads to enraged obsessing on their beloved, which mars their thinking, charges their emotions, and guides faulty choices. I had clients who were paralyzed by pining for their beloved; one man totally obsessed about his ex-wife for five years after their breakup, and another woman was totally incapacitated (refusing to date or go on with her life) for years after her lover left her. This stage of PRSD may also include hypervigilant mate guarding, stalking, love suicide, couple suicide, domestic murder, physical and emotional abuse, and battering. People who remain in the instinctual drive of being in-love get fixated on the loss of their "lover," the one who was sent to them, who is their destiny, and the one they "possess" and "own." These people then begin behaviors aimed at reclaiming their spouse, girlfriend, or lover. They stalk the person they owned and, if frustrated, physically abuse them. If nothing else works, they often kill them, and themselves. In Chapter 5, we'll explore some examples of this stage of PRSD.

5

The Malevolent Offspring of Post-Romantic Stress Disorder

Parting is all we need to know of hell.

—Emily Dickinson

As the best wine doth make the sharpest vinegar, so the deepest love turneth to the deadliest hate.

—John Lyly, 1579,
Euphues: The Anatomy of Wit

Alice's rejection of Tom showed me how devastating PRSD can be. The first six weeks were the worst for him. At one point, I thought I'd need to hospitalize him and put him on suicide watch. Tom went in and out of depression for a year after the initial shock of being rejected. Trauma has been described as "frozen grief," and we now know that grief is a unique process for each person, and it takes varying lengths of time to work through it.

Tom was abandoned by his father when he was three years old. He was shame-based and hypervigilant about rejection. When Alice jilted him, if he had not previously done therapeutic work on his unresolved childhood wounds, he might have gone on to exhibit severe behaviors like stalking her, or finding her and killing both himself and her, or physically or emotionally abusing her, or getting revenge by making her and her new husband anxious and uncomfortable.

Tom had become acquainted with Alice's best friend, and he called her daily to check on Alice. I slowly convinced him to stop phoning this person, as the obsessive calling was a kind of stalking.

People who have not done work on their unresolved childhood trauma—what I call their "wounded inner child" or what James Hollis calls the "hauntings from the past"—will have a reduced chance of resolving their PRSD unless they are willing to do the kind of work described in Part II, Chapter 8. It is essentially "grief work," but I also refer to it as "original pain" work.

Unfortunately, many trudge through life in a semi-unconscious state. They believe the past is over; what's done is done. "My childhood was bad," they say, "but I survived it." With that, they move on, unaware of the unconscious wounds that are distorting or destroying their life, and possibly others around them as well.

PLAY MISTY FOR ME

Clint Eastwood produced and starred in a movie entitled *Play Misty for Me*. It's a movie about the stages of stalking and how they grow increasingly dangerous. Eastwood plays a late-night disc jockey named Dave. He is very handsome and is an object upon which angry, lonely, resentful, and wounded people project their desires. Handsome men or beautiful women, especially those who are in the public eye, are often the objects of lustful fantasies. The in-love PEA/dopamine cocktail is enhanced by adversity, distance, danger, and risk. Many emotionally or mentally ill people who lack a sense of solid selfhood try to "complete themselves" by fantasizing that they are having an affair with a powerful figure in their lives.

In *Play Misty for Me*, a woman named Evelyn (played by Jessica Walter) is waiting for Dave at the late-night bar he frequents. She tells him she had specifically come there to meet him. She is very sexy and seduces him that night. From that point on, she appears everywhere, most often unexpectedly. The movie does a good job in showing the escalation of her stalking delusion and how Dave aids in fueling her fire by succumbing to her overt offers of sex. Slowly, the mystery of sexy Evelyn, who called requesting Dave play the song "Misty" at the end of the evening, turns into a nightmare.

As the film progresses, Dave rekindles the fires of love with an old girlfriend, which sets off Evelyn's severe jealousy. She stalks both Dave and his girlfriend and becomes increasingly violent. Evelyn is clearly unstable emotionally, even mentally ill, and she wants Dave at any cost. She ransacks his home, tries to murder the housekeeper, and then tries to kill herself in his apartment. In the end she attempts to murder Dave and his true lover.

Play Misty for Me is a malevolent love story. Contrary to the love stories I mentioned in Chapter 1, this one touches on the cold, hard reality of PRSD and stalking. Before I give you examples of the violent behavior of people I actually counseled or knew, let's examine the unique characteristic of being in-love that is the major source of these malevolent love behaviors.

ANGER (RAGE) AND REJECTION

A poem, *Pent-Up Aching Rivers* by Walt Whitman, expresses the inherent aspect of being in-love that has such dangerous potential. He writes:

I LOVE YOU, O YOU ENTIRELY POSSESS ME,
O THAT YOU AND I ESCAPE FROM THE REST AND GO UTTERLY
OFF, FREE AND LAWLESS . . .

The poem expresses the lover's desire for absolute "exclusivity" with their lover. During the romance "trance," the lovers feel that they belong to each other. They believe they possess and own each other. They are jealous of any looking or talking about another person of the opposite sex. They feel that fate, or a higher power (God), or life's mysterious forces have put them together. Being together is their destiny. For couples who are in-love, being together (for many "being *alone* together") is all they care about.

Therefore, when the low-T partner begins to withdraw sexually, their high-T partner feels betrayed and abandoned. This is not the case with every high-T partner, but it's usually true of the ones who are highly shame-based and carrying a lot of wounds and/or developmental dependency need deficits from the past. Even those who are healthy can feel an intense loss when a relationship breaks up. They have given their very "being" to their partner. One client told me, for instance, "I told her everything about me. I held nothing back." Another described it as being completely and utterly naked, with no defenses.

This fairly well defines the experience of shame and trauma— being in a powerless state with no way to defend yourself. Add to this feeling of shame the absolute belief that you possess and own the person who is leaving you, and you have entered the mind of the stalker.

From the point of view of brain chemistry, a cherished experience (amazing sex) is being taken away. This partly explains the anger (rage) the rejected one expresses. Anger is the emotion that fuels action. When divorce occurs (especially for a mother with a child or children), anger helps prepare the person for reentry into the mating world.

MAUREEN: LOVE SUICIDE

Less violent forms of stalking can escalate into violence against one's beloved or one's self. Maureen, one of my former clients, was the spitting image of Elizabeth Taylor. She went berserk when her lover Mark went back to Maybell, the woman he was courting before he fell for the exceptionally beautiful Maureen. Maureen called the old girlfriend several hours at night, and also during the day when she knew she was home. She'd hang up the phone the moment Maybell answered. As the in-love passion between Mark and Maybell intensified, Maureen became more desperate, covering Maybell's car with ketchup several times and, on one occasion, slashing her tires. I was not able to stop her, so I referred her to a psychiatrist friend of mine who had experience with intensely passionate ex-lovers. He used medication to quiet her down.

A short time later, my psychiatrist friend called me to report that Maureen had gotten married! Only three months had passed since she stopped taunting Maybell. About a year and a half later, I learned that Maureen had gained a lot of weight. When she met Mark, she was a svelte 115 pounds—now she tipped the scales at 375 pounds! Ultimately, she was hospitalized for obesity and died a year later. You could easily say that Maureen's PRSD led to suicide by food; she committed "love suicide."

SID'S STORY:
LOVE SUICIDE AND MURDER

I had a client for two years who was one of the gentlest men I've ever interacted with. I'll call him Sid. Sid came to me because he wanted to be heterosexual, even though for a major part of his sex life he had been homosexual. Strangely, the only decent relationship he'd been in was with the woman he was currently engaged to. While they did not have a vibrant sex life, they did occasionally make love with a high degree of satisfaction. Sid was clearly gay, but a counselor learns that coming out of the closet is an extremely private matter. It can't be rushed, cajoled, or bribed by a therapist—or by the religious people who spout their judgment and scorn on people like Sid.

Sid frequently went out late at night to gay establishments where booths are set up and men watch porn and have oral sex through peepholes. (Heterosexuals also have variations on these kinds of bars.) When Sid returned from one of his late-night outings, he called me and sobbed uncontrollably. He felt terrible about himself. Talking to him on the phone made it clear that Sid was fighting to be heterosexual, but he was going against his God-given biological inheritance. The whole experience of being in sex clubs is shaming for both gays and heterosexuals.

One night his fiancée, Linda, heard him get up to go out, so she followed him. She was shocked and hurt by what she observed. But it gave us a chance to deal with Sid's issues in therapy. Many women would have ended the relationship right then and there, but Linda loved Sid unconditionally and, despite the obvious challenges, hoped to make it work between the two of them. She wanted honesty and openness from Sid in exchange for her understanding. Linda had made a contract with Sid that she would end their engagement if Sid acted out without sharing his needs with her. This was certainly reasonable, and I thought we were making some progress in my sessions with Sid.

Then one day I got some terrible news. Linda called and told me that Sid had shot himself in the head! She confronted him when he returned home from yet another sex shop. A few hours later, Sid went to his garage and killed himself! In all my years of counseling, I've never known of any gay man or lesbian woman who became successfully heterosexual. Sid was ultimately conflicted. He couldn't admit to his impulses, and he was highly ashamed of his gay bar behavior, yet he couldn't stop going. He felt he needed Linda's love to survive, and knowing that he couldn't live up to their contract, he chose to die rather than live without her.

THE EXPERT GEOLOGIST:
A CASE OF "DOMESTIC MURDER"

One of the strangest experiences of my life took place when I was the director of human resources for an oil company in 1979. One of the prospective geologists we needed to evaluate came to me for testing. We had an extensive system of tests and evaluations that we put a potential worker through before hiring them, especially someone who would be in our geological department. Gilbert passed with flying colors. His scientific knowledge was superb, and while he seemed a bit high-strung emotionally, I attributed this to his Latino passion. Gilbert was hired.

Dr. Bosarge, our CEO, initiated a counseling program for our employees soon after Gilbert was hired. He allowed workers who were in need to have a limited number of private sessions of counseling with me.

Gilbert came to see me because he wanted to talk about his live-in common-law wife, Priscilla. He had met her when she was seventeen and he was forty-two. He fell madly in-love with her, although she only slowly reciprocated these feelings. When Priscilla was nineteen, Gilbert talked her into living with him. When I counseled them, they had been living together for twelve years.

Gilbert wanted me to counsel them both because Priscilla wanted out of the relationship. When I counseled her separately, I concluded that she had finally grown up and seen that the world was much larger than the prison-like world that Gilbert kept her in—and which she initially allowed by letting him control her life. Her thinking had to be exactly like his. Gilbert left detailed instructions outlining what she should do each day.

She was responsible for all the housework and grocery shopping. Gilbert demanded that she be ready for sex twice a day, whenever he was in the mood. First, he had his daily blow job at noon. He had even convinced Priscilla of the nutritional value of his sperm. She was to be bathed and perfumed each evening by eight o'clock. This was in preparation for two hours of intercourse. Priscilla reported that she was rarely ever satisfied and had gradually come to experience Gilbert as downright repulsive.

During a second session, I saw clearly his need to keep her under his complete control. He ordered her to return two blouses she had purchased—stating that they were too sexy! At a third session, when she expressed her desire to go home and visit her family and friends, Gilbert went berserk. His behavior was so bizarre I had to get our CEO's permission to have him committed for seventy-two hours.

When I talked to Priscilla alone, she expressed her true feelings. It was clear that she was extremely co-dependent, afraid of going it alone, and fearful of Gilbert's rage. She said that she no longer loved him and that their sex life was over. When I saw them again two weeks later, Gilbert turned his wrath onto me, demeaning my counseling skills and saying he was going to find another therapist. I was going on a ten-day vacation at this time and asked him to think things over while I was gone. I asked Gilbert and Priscilla to make a "no contact" contract until I could see them one more time. I somehow convinced Gilbert to reluctantly agree.

When I returned from my vacation the first thing I did was call the geology department to check on Gilbert. I was stunned to hear that five nights earlier Gilbert had gotten a shotgun and killed Priscilla and then himself. We often hear reports of domestic homicide on the news or reports of heinous stories of a man killing his wife and/or family prior to killing himself. But to be as intimately involved as I was in Gilbert and Priscilla's story devastated me. I kept thinking about Priscilla, how she had, in effect, had her life stolen and become Gilbert's prisoner for more than a dozen years.

Fisher's discovery of the brain chemistry program of a person in-love (the romance program), with its production of dopamine, norepinephrine, and the reduction of serotonin, helped me understand the crazed chemical behavior that motivated Gilbert—but it didn't help much. The home, the marriage, and the place where we want to belong and find refuge and nourishment can be the most dangerous place on Earth.

As Judith Barwick puts it in her book, *In Transition*, "Marriage and this family are where we live out our most intimate and powerful human experiences. The family is the unit in which we belong, from which we can expect protection from uncontrollable fate, in which we create infinity through our children, and in which we find a haven. The stuff that family is made of is bloodier and more passionate than the stuff of friendship and the costs are greater too."

There are many more examples of this malevolent form of PRSD. One of the most infamous was that of NFL football legend O. J. Simpson who, in 1995, was acquitted of murdering his ex-wife Nicole and her friend Ron Goldman. The Simpsons had a tempestuous relationship, peppered with infidelity and domestic violence, which resulted in their divorce.

Later, a civil trial concluded that O. J. Simpson had wrongfully caused the death of his ex-wife and her innocent friend. Although Nicole was no longer his wife, O. J. still had his in-love chemicals of ownership. He felt he possessed his ex-wife, and the insane jealousy triggered by the chemicals that were operative in the romance program allowed him to feel that no one else should ever have Nicole.

Certain shame-based people with low self-esteem begin to feel severely threatened when they feel that their once-fantastic love is out of their *control*. Even after a divorce, even if they have moved on to another relationship, they still feel the all-embracing exclusivity, the sense of owning and possessing their ex-wives.

It is more common for men to stalk, threaten, and harass the lovers who have left them. Those who are less violent steal jewelry and underwear. An incident in Texas, however, shows the gruesome extent to which some men will go without actually killing their beloved. A headline in the *Houston Chronicle* (March 25, 2014), read: "Beheaded Dog Charges Lead to Stalking Charges Against Ex-Boyfriend." Christopher Forkah mutilated and decapitated his ex-girlfriend's ten-year-old dog. He also assaulted her several times, although she failed to report him. He left warnings in blood and threatened to kill her.

EMOTIONAL TUG-OF-WAR: JEALOUSY VERSUS ABANDONMENT

Shakespeare wrote this about jealousy:

O, BEWARE, MY LORD, OF JEALOUSY;
IT IS THE GREEN-EY'D MONSTER, WHICH DOTH MOCK
THE MEAT IT FEEDS ON. THAT CUCKOLD LIVES IN BLISS,
WHO, CERTAIN OF HIS FATE, LOVES NOT HIS WRONGER:
BUT O, WHAT DAMNED MINUTES TELLS HE O'ER
WHO DOTES, YET DOUBTS, SUSPECTS, YET STRONGLY LOVES!

(Othello 3.3.165–71)

Jealousy is not only universal, but actually has a biological imperative and is common in all of nature. Scientists call it "mate guarding," and it evolved to discourage a mate from deserting the family unit and thus give the young a better chance of survival. While low-level jealousy might make one partner more attentive to the other, higher degrees of jealousy can result in domestic violence. Oftentimes, the jealousy is irrational and unfounded.

I counseled a woman whose husband used to beat her during sex because he told her he knew she was fantasizing about having sex with someone else. She swore to him that she was not, but nothing she said or did would satisfy him. She eventually divorced him, but she didn't feel safe even then, and moved two thousand miles across the country to escape his rage.

Men have great fears of being tricked or cuckolded; women more often have fears of abandonment. Women are often more tolerant of a man's one-night stand but won't stand by silently if they find evidence of their husband's emotional attachment to another woman. Fisher believes this may be a behavior that makes Darwinian sense, since women need mates to help them rear their young.

Jealousy seems like it would be a death knell to a love affair, but many psychologists believe it can move a mate to make strong overtures of nurturing and prove their fidelity and attachment. In my clinical experience, however, I found jealousy to be a negative factor in all my clients' love relationships. Contrary to what some have said, I did not find that jealousy motivated either partner to change their behavior for the better. Instead, many only did so in order to manipulate their partner—most often doing something they really disliked!

NONVIOLENT STALKING:
A PERSONAL EXPERIENCE

Violence as a result of stalking is what usually makes the headlines, but there are other nonviolent forms that are prevalent and dangerous. While men are the main offenders, women also stalk. I can attest to this from personal experience. During the first ten years of my counseling practice, I had two different women stalkers who gave me a great deal of trouble. Clients often fall in-love with their counselor. This is why therapists must be so careful about what is referred to as "countertransference." In my case, I had terminated one woman's counseling sessions with me. I felt that she resisted the things that would clearly help her. This woman fairly quickly began to appear everywhere I went. I began to find roses on my car, and even flowers at the door of my home. Then she appeared at out-of-town events.

I confronted her many times, using firm and unequivocal language. She justified her behavior, saying that she was a Ph.D. student and was learning from me. The notes she left, however, became more and more sexual. Her behavior did not let up, and the stalking continued for five years. She finally moved to the northwest part of the United States and stopped stalking me. Still, I was anxious about her for a long time, and I feared she might destroy my family, although I never resorted to getting a restraining order.

Another woman stalked me by mail. I'd never seen or met her. At the time, I was doing a lot of specials on PBS and facilitating workshops all over the country. She must've seen me on television, attended a workshop, and/or read my books, because she was very familiar with my life and work.

Every week, I received two letters from this woman, who was the minister of a church in Oklahoma. The letters were religious but also graphic with subtle promises of sexual pleasures I'd purportedly never dreamed of. At first I found the letters curious and even amusing. I finally wrote her back expressing my marital commitment and my absolute disinterest in having any relationship with her—divine, human, or animal. This tactic backfired, as I discovered that any letter I sent—some finally outright insulting—triggered even more passionate responses. The feeling of being in-love is enhanced by adversity.

Realizing this and not wanting the situation to escalate, I stopped responding to her correspondence. Still, it was two years later when she finally stopped writing.

These behaviors, while seemingly nonviolent, are in fact a form of violence. They threatened my family and caused me great emotional suffering. The offenders had a complete disregard for my boundaries, and I was a victim, even though I was never physically harmed.

SURPRISING STALKING STATISTICS

Stalking is hardly the domain of the uneducated offender. Fisher cites one study of American college students where 34 percent of women said they had been stalked by men they had rejected. College males are also stalked by females, but the percentage is not fully known. Beyond higher education, the U.S. Justice Department reports that every year more than a million American women are stalked. Sixty percent are stalked by boyfriends, husbands, former spouses, or live-in partners.

PHYSICALLY ABUSIVE PARTNERS

Men also batter women. One third of all women seeking emergency medical care, one out of four women who attempt suicide, and some 20 percent of pregnant women who seek prenatal care have been battered by an intimate partner. The number of battered women is probably far more than we know because of the fear of reporting such incidences.

I've had three women knock on my door in the early morning hours in order to escape their husband's beatings, two of them with tiny babies. In these cases, I have been able to help them arrange restraining orders until some help could be provided.

Two of these couples have had successful treatment at The Meadows treatment center in Wickenburg, Arizona. Both of the male batterers were medical doctors, and very elitist and controlling. This is no indictment of the medical profession or doctors. It is more a description of the elements of abusive, male wife beaters. These shameless offenders cross all cultures and socioeconomic boundaries. They are emotionally sick people who believe they *own* their wives. While their victims often feel that they caused the problem, that maybe there is something they should be doing differently, professional intervention by a trained mental health clinician can be very helpful.

As I shared in my story about Gilbert, the engineer, men kill their beloveds too. According to Fisher, about "32 percent of all female murder victims in the United States die at the hands of spouses, ex-spouses, boyfriends and ex-boyfriends, but other experts believe that the true numbers may be as high as 50 to 70 percent. Over 50 percent of these murderers stalk their lovers first."

Being in-love or rather, in the romance program, while longed for and desired by many young men and women, can tragically end in fourth-degree malevolent PRSD, one of the most dangerous behaviors that flow from our genetic inheritance.

PART II

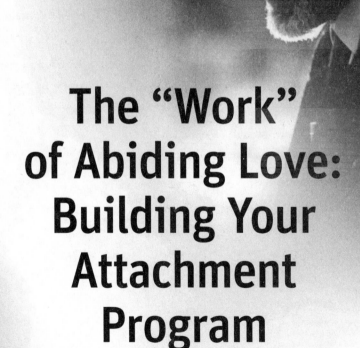

The "Work" of Abiding Love: Building Your Attachment Program

Seldom, or perhaps never,
does a marriage develop into an individual
relationship smoothly and without crisis;
there is no coming to consciousness
without pain.

—Carl Jung

PROLOGUE:
"HOPE SPRINGS"

So you're not in-love, but you do love your spouse. Without being condescending, let me say, "Yeah! That's the way nature intended it." As I've described in Part I, being in-love evolved to move our ancient ancestors to find and pursue a specific mating partner. This started the mating process and helped ensure remaining sexually faithful to each other long enough to have the possibility of offspring, and to care for them, which would extend both partners' DNA.

After settling down and deciding to have a child, or getting pregnant first and deciding to keep the child (quite common in my experience), a new brain program is initiated; a new set of chemicals and a new brain circuitry is established. As we previously discussed, the new program is called "attachment." Feelings of attachment dampen the romance and lust programs and replace them with a sense of connection, warmth, and security.

In order to deepen our attachment program and expand it into an intimate connection and commitment, we have "work" to do! Being in-love is spontaneous. Achieving a fully adult kind of mature love takes effort. It involves humility, docility, and at times hard work.

LONG-TERM MARRIAGE

One of the best movies I've seen is entitled Hope Springs, *starring Meryl Streep and Tommy Lee Jones. It is an example of a thirty-year marriage completely stuck in the third degree of PRSD. It is the kind of love story that shows us what can happen in a long-term marriage if a couple does no work to deepen their love. Kay (Meryl Streep) and Arnold (Tommy Lee Jones) are a late-middle-aged couple who find themselves in a declining marriage, to the point where they are now sleeping in separate rooms. Kay finds a book by a man named Dr. Feld (Steve Carell) who conducts expensive weeklong sessions in a small town in Maine called Great Hope Springs. She has saved the money from her job at a retail store to pay for it and convinces her reluctant husband to visit. Great Hope Springs is a place where the couple can work together to invigorate their sexless marriage and renew and revitalize their marital commitment—or find*

*out if they are so stuck that probably neither partner is
really going to change.*

*The therapy that Jones's and Streep's characters go
through is as real as anything I've ever seen or worked
with in my practice. Arnold is a hardworking middle-
class man who is fearful and paranoid about being ripped
off. He has a low degree of solid selfhood. As the movie
progresses, we also see how angry he is and how passive-
aggressive she is. Arnold engages Dr. Feld in a power
struggle from the get-go, shaming him for being a therapist and for ripping everyone off with his outrageous
fees. At two points in their therapy sessions, he simply
walks out—both times when Dr. Feld confronts him on
something he could handle if only his self-identity were
stronger. As with many people with a fuzzy sense of self,
he runs away from conflict.*

*Kay tells the therapist that she is very unhappy, and
says, "We never talk about anything." What she didn't
know was that she and Arnold had covertly agreed upon
"no-talk" and "no-feel" rules in their marriage, which
are fairly universal in unhappy relationships. They come
from the parental injunction that says, "If you can't say
something nice, don't say anything it at all." The rule
forbids talking about problems—which are never "nice."
The fact is, you can talk about problems when your sense
of self is strong enough to bear discomfort for the sake
of growth.*

Kay says she feels like their marriage is about two people who go to work every day and bunk together every night. She tells the therapist that, ironically, she would be less lonely if she were alone! We soon learn that they've been sexless for years. *When the therapist asks, "When is the last time you had sex?" Arnold says, "I have no idea!" Kay thinks for a moment and then gives a date,* five *years earlier. But we learn that what sex they have had was mostly uncreative and a static routine—always in the missionary position. Kay has made a courageous move to get Arnold to go to therapy with her; nevertheless, her sense of self is on shaky ground.*

IT TAKES TWO TO TANGO

If I had to wager, I would bet that most people viewing this movie would view Arnold as the problem. He's the most combative and resistant to change, or even to discussion. It is less obvious that Kay is at least 50 percent responsible. She is extremely co-dependent *and (until therapy) never tells Tom about her dislikes, feelings, and needs. Dr. Feld asks them both to share their sexual fantasies. Arnold admits that one of his was for Kay to perform oral sex on him. When the therapist asks Kay about oral sex, she makes a face and says she finds it distasteful.*

The therapist assigns them exercises that range from holding and touching, to oral sex, and later to having intercourse. They attempt to do the exercises but with no real success. The therapist tells Arnold that Kay could really divorce him when they get home. He tells Arnold that she has developed enough selfhood to refuse a dead-end, lifeless marriage. The thought of this shakes Arnold into action, so he arranges for a romantic dinner and books a fancy room for Kay and him to spend the night. After having dinner, they go up to their hotel room and become very romantic; they get excited but just can't finish the job. It becomes clear that Kay is very frightened sexually, and they cannot complete their conjugal tasks.

Discouraged, they end their therapy sessions and leave Great Hope Springs. Back home, we see them fall into their old routine—sleeping in separate bedrooms and Arnold parked in his recliner every night watching the Golf Channel—until Kay decides to leave! She's got her bags packed when, unexpectedly, Arnold knocks on her bedroom door. His assertive sexual body language moves her, and they engage in passionate sex. A day later, Arnold rushes to go to work, but then stops on his way out the front door and comes back to give Kay a wild sexual kiss, while fondling her body. Kay loves it!

At the end of the movie, they are back in Great Hope Springs, having a renewal ceremony of their marriage vows. Some of the vows are quite personal and specific,

*like Kay vowing to watch more golf on TV and Arnold
promising to watch golf less. Golf was one of their "dis-
connects." Their children are their witnesses, along with
their therapist, Dr. Feld, who is the officiate presiding
over the ceremony. It ends with the breaking of a mold of
a nose. This is significant because Dr. Feld had compared
their marriage to a "deviated septum," where neither
could breathe freely. They had lost any real spontaneity.
The therapist used the deviated septum metaphor to help
them understand that to heal the nose it must be broken!
Kay's decision to actually leave is equivalent to "breaking the nose" in the metaphor.*

*Several very helpful statements came out of this movie
that touch on a lot of issues people face in a long-term
relationship. I highly encourage you to rent the movie,
then ask yourself the following questions:*

- *While I might feel I am right about something,
  what is worth more to me—my partner or my
  pride?*
- *Is standing on principle really more important
  than my relationship?*
- *Have I done all that I could to be a good partner
  and work at my marriage?*
- *What can I do to renew and invigorate my
  marriage?*

There are probably things we'd all like to change about our partners, but you must be willing to change yourself first. This requires being willing to develop a stronger sense of self. As marriage slowly gets in a rut, the partners become blinded by the routines they get stuck in. When this happens, each partner feels cut off and alone.

The therapist in Hope Springs *told Arnold and Kay that they were at a serious impasse. In using the deviated septum as a metaphor for their stuck marriage, he makes it clear that to get it unstuck, the nose must be broken, and breaking a nose* does not happen slowly. *You have to act your way into feeling like you want to change, and often do what you do not want to do.*

6

Three More New Discoveries!

"The brain is wider than the sky."
—Emily Dickinson

"The exertion of willful effort generates a physical force that has the power to change how the brain works and its physical structure."
—Jeffrey Schwartz and Sharon Begley,
The Mind and the Brain

"Without the amplification of feeling (affects) nothing matters and with their amplification anything can matter."
—Silvan Tomkins,
Affect, Imagery, and Consciousness

I n my own early stages of recovery from alcoholism, I was in a recovery meeting and I heard a guy say, "In order to change, I had to act myself into a right way of thinking and feeling rather than wait until I thought clearly and felt like doing what I needed to do to change." When we have a low sense of self and are in a rut, we generally feel safe and secure in the rut. It's more comfortable to go along with the status quo even if it is unhealthy. When we are in the rut, we might feel frozen—our actions are mostly unconscious—so that we can't think or feel like doing the things necessary for real change to take place. We very often need outside help to understand.

In my later years of counseling, I made a very strong contract with the person I was treating. I'd say, "You've come to me in emotional pain. You don't know how to stop your distress. If you knew what to do you wouldn't need me. So whatever I insist you do, you do it, whether you understand it or not. If you don't do what I ask you to do, I'll stop the counseling." Many therapists might find this contract clinically incorrect, but I had a lot of success when a client agreed to it. In fact, those who agreed to the contract indeed changed. How could they *desire* to do something when they came to me with a "desire" problem—resulting from each partner's lack of solid selfhood?

Couples are usually stuck when they reach out for help. The things they might have to do are out of their comfort zone. As the old adage says, "Nothing changes until *something* changes." Often you must change what you are doing and not worry about what your partner does or doesn't do. If you change your behavior, there will be a pattern interruption, which allows a space for your partner to change. I'll assure you that both partners must take it as their obligation to risk building a stronger sense of self. As you work through Part II of this book, be willing to be an adult and put away your score-keeping "childishness."

We almost always want to wait, but love means action. Small pattern interruptions can begin by taking action, even if you don't fully understand why the new action can be so effective. Fortunately, new discoveries about "willpower" and the brain explain why "acting yourself" into a right way of thinking and feeling works so well.

NEW DISCOVERIES ABOUT CHANGING RELATIONSHIPS

The first two of the last three new discoveries that have increased our knowledge about changing relationships are directly related to changing behavior. The third is a breakthrough concerning the emotional health of every human being, and therefore of healthy relationships.

THE NEUROPLASTICITY OF THE BRAIN

Dr. Jeffrey Schwartz, a professor of psychiatry at the UCLA School of Medicine, defines neuroplasticity as "the ability of neurons to forge new connections, to blaze new paths through the cortex." In layman's terms, neuroplasticity means rewiring the brain. This new truth exploded the long-held belief that once the brain reached maturity in late adolescence, it cannot be changed.

In his book *The Mind and the Brain: Neuroplasticity and the Power of Mental Force*, with award-winning science columnist Sharon Begley, Schwartz presented his experimental research with obsessive compulsive (OCD) patients. He took PET scans of their brains before and after his experimental treatment (a ten-week program). In some cases, after finishing their treatment, the OCD patients showed as much as an 80 percent change in the part of the brain responsible for their compulsivity. The before-and-after PET scans showed a dramatic shrinkage in the size of the brain area known as the right caudate nucleus. This decrease in size indicated that the energy circulating between the right caudate, the right orbitofrontal cortex, and the right thalamus had been interrupted. What this means is that a rigid and seemingly automatic process of obsessing on something and feeling compelled to take action had been disrupted. Schwartz says, "Willful effort generates a *physical force* that has the power to change how the brain works and even its physical structure" (p. 18; for a summary of Schwartz's work, see my book *Reclaiming Virtue* [Chapter 3, pp. 89–120]).

Lest the implications of this discovery pass you by, think of places you are "stuck" in your marriage, how you obsess or negatively and automatically act a certain way—your wife constantly criticizes you, so you refuse to share feelings or anything else with her. You complain that she bitches and nags all the time; she complains that you won't talk (share your feelings, listen to her needs, etc.). The fact is, you each cause the other's behavior and keep each other from growing a more solid sense of self. As Sir Isaac Newton's third law of physics states, "For every action there is an equal and opposite reaction."

The popular brain expert Dr. Daniel J. Siegel has shown how the mind itself is the product of interpersonal experience. In his book *The Developing Mind: How Relationships and the Brain Interact to Shape Who We Are,* Siegel writes, "The mind emerges from the activity of the brain, whose structure and function are directly shaped by interpersonal experience."

CINDY AND ROBERT: A RELATIONSHIP STUCK ON THE SPIN CYCLE

Cindy and Robert were stuck in a vicious cycle that spun their relationship nowhere. Cindy was constantly criticizing Robert about even inconsequential things. When I asked her why, she answered, "Because he won't share and talk." When I asked Robert why he wouldn't share and talk, he said, "Because Cindy criticizes me all the time."

It was a classic case of the "bitch and nag/won't discuss anything" cycle. This couple's brains are grooved in such a way that each one creates the other's behavior, and both stay in a childish standoff. Think of a car, stuck in the mud. If you press on the accelerator, the tires spin into a rut. If you press harder on the pedal, thinking you will get out of the rut, guess what happens? You are still stuck there, and the rut has gotten deeper. Doing the same thing will get you nowhere, and the same can be said of a relationship.

If you believe you are in a rut, one of you needs to change, and it doesn't matter who it is (unless you are being abused). If one person changes their behavior, it can change the other person. One of you needs to just use your will and do it! I'll come back to this time after time in this part of the book. Take responsibility—act yourself into changing your marriage. Act yourself into a stronger sense of self. Amazingly, one of you can engineer the whole thing. But you have to stop keeping score!

Schwartz's work clearly establishes the existence, character, and casual efficacy of the will. He has rediscovered willpower, showing that "directed, willed mental activity can clearly and systematically alter brain function." The exertion of "willful effort" generates a "physical force" on your brain, and it works.

I can personally attest to this. December 11, 2014, marks forty-nine years for me without a drink of alcohol. When I read Schwartz's work, it was clear why acting myself into a right way of thinking worked. When I acted, I was using my will as a physical force to change my brain.

THE PRIMACY OF THE AFFECT
(FEELING) SYSTEM

Since the time of Descartes, philosophers have emphasized reason, thinking, and analytic logic over willpower and emotion. At this point in human history, willpower is being restored, and so are feelings. In the last quarter of the twentieth century, a psychologist named Silvan Tomkins presented his theory of the primacy of the affect system. By observing his baby and those of others, he concluded that the commonly held opinion that crying is the result of thinking was wrong. He determined that babies just cry. They have no reasons that trigger sadness. Babies are just innately happy, curious, angry, fearful, sad, and shameful.

Tomkins found nine innate affects (feelings) that are biological mechanisms that unfold according to precisely written biological programs. The last two affects he found were "dissmell" and disgust (affects that protect us from toxic air, water, and food). As our sense of self evolves, dissmell and disgust move beyond biological protection and become a part of our emotional self-protection system (we will explore this in more detail in Chapter 9).

When we are aware of an affect, we call it a feeling. Tomkins found that each affect (feeling) has its own unique facial expression and vocalization (see Figure 6.1). Tomkins's nine innate affects (feelings) were verified by psychologists Paul Ekman and Carroll Izard. They showed pictures of the facial expressions of the nine affects in twenty-one countries and found that they were universally recognized.

Figure 6.1:
Tomkins's Nine Innate Affects (Feelings)

Positive Affects:

Enjoyment/Joy: physically smiling, lips wide and out

Interest/Excitement: physically, eyebrows are down, eyes are tracking and looking, and there is closer listening

Neutral Affects:

Surprise/Startle: physically, eyebrows are up and eyes are blinking

Negative Affects:

Anger/Rage: physically, the face is frowning and red, and the jaw is clenched

Fear/Terror: physically, the face is pale with a frozen stare that exhibits coldness and sweating, and the hair may be erect

Shame/Humiliation: physically, the eyes are lowered, the head is down and averted, and the face may be blushing

Distress/Anguish: person is physically crying with rhythmic sobbing, eyebrows are arched, and the mouth is lowered

Dissmell (reaction to bad smell): physically, the upper lip is raised and the head is pulled back

Disgust: physically, the lower lip is raised and protruding while the head is forward and down

Tomkins went on to show that the nine affects (feelings) were an interacting system. He further saw affect as "the primary motivator of human behavior." In his oft-quoted statement, he said, "I see affect (feeling) as the primary innate biological motivating mechanism, more urgent than drive deprivation and pleasure, and more urgent even than physical pain." He made it clinically clear that without the amplification of feelings (affects), nothing matters, and with their amplification, anything can matter. Affects (our feelings) are the blueprint for cognition, desire, decision, and action. In my own recovery program, the more I owned and expressed my feelings, the more I moved away from my thinking denials and faulty choices. Feelings are the old brain's way of thinking. The importance of the feeling system is at least five-fold:

- Nothing matters without feelings.
- We cannot make a decision without feelings.
  Choice itself is at stake when we have numbed out
  and repressed our feelings.
- We cannot think without feelings.
- Feelings are the primary motivators of human behavior.
- We cannot be intimate without expressing feelings.

This last point has the most relevance for our creating a mature love with our spouses. Intimacy involves vulnerability, and we are never more vulnerable than when expressing our feelings. Both partners must learn to express their feelings, as sharing feelings is one of the unique opportunities we have to be intimate.

7

Realistic Expectations

Perfection would not be enough.

—Carl Rogers

Where there is life, there is strife.

—Anonymous

The great therapist Carl Rogers was once asked what he did to prepare himself to do a session of therapy with a client. Rogers is said to have answered, "I tell myself that I'm enough. I'm not perfect, because perfection would not be enough." Rogers insisted that whatever his client told him, he would be able to understand it because his client is human. Echoing the Roman philosopher Seneca, who said, "Nothing human is foreign to me," Rogers felt he was *adequate*. He was not perfect because, as he says, "If we were perfect, we would not be human. Perfect would not be enough." We may be able to get a perfect score on an exam created by another human being, but we can *never* be perfect *in our very being*. Why? Because as human beings we are, as we say at The Meadows treatment center, "perfectly imperfect."

One of our innate affects is shame, which is the maker of our finitude. We are the animals who *blush*, because we are the animals who can and will make mistakes. We make a huge mistake when we try to be *more than human*, that is, when we try to act shameless and be perfect. Chart 7A is an adaptation from my book *Healing the Shame That Binds You* (revised edition, p. 27).

Chart 7A:
Dynamics of the Affect Shame

Shameless	Shame	Shameless
Less Than Human "Neurotic"	An Innate Affect That Marks Our Finitude and Forms Our Sense of Self Just Human	More Than Human "Character Disordered"
Wholly Imperfect To Blame for Everything	"Perfectly Imperfect" Self-Responsible	Perfect Not to Blame for Any Mess-ups

Letting Go of Control	Balance Between Holding On and Letting Go	Holding On— Trying to Stay in Control All the Time
Power Through Failure	Power Thru Virtue Serenity Prayer*	A False Sense of POWER
Confessing Defects with Little or No Boundaries	Appropriately Vulnerable Semi-Permeable Boundaries	Invulnerable Rigid Boundaries
Underfunctioning Curiositas Knows Nothing "I Am a Mistake"	Fully Functional Self Docility Still Learning Mistakes Are My Teachers	Over-Functioning Prideful Know It All No Mistakes
Anger As Rage	Anger As Boundary	Passive Aggressive Anger
To Blame for Everything	Responsible for Self and Behaviors	Never to Blame for Anything
Compulsive: Eating Spending Drinking Alcohol/Drugs Bingeing	Moderation In: Eating Spending Drinking Alcohol/Drugs	Compulsive: Dieting Saving Temperance Alcohol/Drugs
Totally Flawed and Defective A Sinner Resigned to Damnation	God As I Understand— Humble, Being Nobody Special	Authoritarian God Elitist Know I'm Saved

*AA uses the Serenity Prayer—"God grant me the serenity to accept the things I cannot change, help me to change the things I can and give me the wisdom to know the difference." It is believed that the theologian Reinhold Niebuhr first said this.

Shame safeguards our boundaries and our limitations. Shame especially monitors two other innate affects: *interest/ curiosity* and *excitement/joy* (celebration). When we feel shame, it is like a tap on our shoulder that says, "That's enough fun and enough curiosity." Shame is the core of the medieval vice *curiositas*, which says in effect that you can "get on your horse and ride off in *all directions*." We need structure and boundaries in order to be truly free.

Shame is a healthy marker of our limitations, and having a boundary of limitations is a healthy asset. But to grow up with parents who are shameless—who have violated you physically (chronic spankings), sexually (incest, covert or overt), emotionally (chronic shaming of your whole being), intellectually (making fun of your thoughts and ideas), spiritually (forcing you to accept dogmatic statements and demanding absolute obedience to that dogma)—forces you to carry on *their* shame.

Once a child has the shame passed to them, the child becomes *shame-based*. Shame is no longer a feeling; it is an *identity*. The "carried shame" is internalized and becomes *toxic shame*. A toxically shame-based person either feels flawless or defective. They fear exposure, so they hide behind the *more than* human behaviors; or, as Chart 7A shows, they may just give up and become the "Best Worst," the bottom of being less than human.

When I first sobered up, I tried to become the Best Worst Drunk. My talks at meetings became drunkalogues. For example, when I was first sobering up, I told my audiences that I walked eight miles in the cold snow to buy whiskey! Today, I would say, "I walked five blocks in the snow." The exaggerated detail is a kind of reverse grandiosity. Because my shame-based self felt flawed and defective as a human being, I tried to be *more than human.* Many others just succumb to being *less than human.* Shame loves hiding and silence. When a person is shamed, they can't breathe and have trouble speaking. Being shame-based makes it extraordinarily hard to let yourself be seen. It is even harder to express feelings. This is why a shame-based person has trouble telling the truth about their vulnerability. The most important impact of toxic shame is its effect on our sense of self. No affect contributes more to the formation of solid selfhood; and when toxic, no affect is more destructive to our sense of self.

In his book *Shame and Pride*, Dr. Donald Nathanson offers an insightful exploration of how shame produces painful self-awareness at every stage of human development. Writing about the infant, Nathanson says, "Shame is the great undoing of whatever has been exciting and pleasurable" (p. 211) to the child. The shame disruption forces the child to evaluate their sense of identity and reevaluate it. In this way shame continually enhances the child's growing awareness of their self (pp. 206–11).

Psychologists in general have accepted Carl Rogers's philosophy of using the phrase "good enough" to describe high-quality behavior. No professional uses the word "perfect" to describe a marriage, family, husband, or wife. The purpose of our innate affect called shame is to monitor our curiosity and pleasure and to let us know we can and will make mistakes. Innate shame is the ground of our finitude; it is our permission to be human. As humans, we make mistakes, need help at times, and have a lot to learn.

Movies, stories, and television shows have presented a picture of married couples and families who think alike, never get bored, argue—but in a comedic way—never feel lonely, never get angry, and share all responsibilities. Strangely, we have no real idea of how they are doing sexually. The assumption is that it is perfect, and everything in their sex life is "rosy." To me the Cosbys, Bradys, and all the rest seem completely sexless and Barbie-like. We know that most of their perfect family behaviors are not true. Such ideas are fanciful and poison us with unrealistic expectations of how it's going to be when we get married.

In this chapter, I've put together a number of realistic expectations for functional, happy marriages. These expectations come from years of working with married couples and families, and from our current level of evolution. I spent several years at Southern Methodist University (SMU) teaching a course to graduate students on marriage and family of origin work. I'm also a senior fellow at The Meadows treatment center in Wickenburg, Arizona, where we treat all forms of addiction, trauma, abuse, and abandonment in the context of a person's whole family system. I'll talk about family a good bit in what follows. The chief component of the family is the marriage. As the marriage goes, so goes the family.

I could begin my list of realistic expectations by stating the opposite of the list I outlined from the movies, novels, fairy tales, and television shows. In fact, people don't always agree, think alike, or want sex equally, and they do get angry and feel lonely. From time to time, any one of us gets caught up in the great "suck of self" that comes from our wounded inner child of the past. Healthy couples experience the disorder of sexual desire in their marriages. Desire, in general, depends on the degree of solid selfhood each partner has achieved. Because each of us is unique and unrepeatable, we are different in many ways. We have true human commonalities, but certainly not in the way the "love stories" suggest.

SOME PROBLEMS WILL NEVER BE FULLY RESOLVED

One of the most prominent figures in the field of love and marriage, John Gottman, cited the research of Andy Christensen, Neil Jacobson, Susan Johnson, Les Greenberg, Doug Snyder, and Dan Wile, all highly respected marital researchers who have concluded that one or more of a couple's marital problems will probably never get fully resolved. Couples who find satisfaction together are those who are willing to compromise and allow their partners to have their differences.

INTIMACY AND DIFFERENCES

Most therapists agree that a couple can become more intimate by truly accepting and understanding their differences. After all, if my partner is exactly like me, what a dull, boring relationship that would be. Another important fact cited by Gottman is that the soaring divorce rate and marital unhappiness is not being helped that much by marital and couples therapy. Only a minority attain a level of non-distress. In a study by researchers Price and Jacobson (1995), only 35 percent of couples receiving marital therapy, using the best-known techniques, reported non-distress. Of those the rate of relapse was 30 to 50 percent over one year.

I can personally attest to the difficulty I had in my beginning work with distressed couples. I probably helped more couples divorce well in the first eight years of my counseling practice. This book is aimed at preventing divorce, but I must say that not all couples should stay together. Helping a couple (usually one person) initiate a divorce is a perfectly valid function of marital therapy. For some couples, therapy is an unconscious way to break up. However, divorce is most often messy, especially if there are one or more children. Divorcing couples with children usually need a therapist to help them with coparenting. In the later years of my practice, from 1978 to 1989 (when I had to stop counseling in order to do my PBS specials and workshops), I had a high percentage of success using the material I will be presenting in the next chapters. Help is available, and we can overcome Post-Romantic Stress Disorder!

In Chart 7B, you can view what I consider the six fundamental problems that have to be dealt with in creating a mature, personalized love between two people. I'll certainly not be able to deal with all of those problems, but I can show those of you who are in trouble ways to change. I'll show you a highly effective way to resolve your conflicts concerning your family of origin's rules and values. I will show you how to resolve many of your differences. Above all, I'll give you a realistic map of the journey you must take when you've resolved your major differences.

In the beginning is the world of "you," in which you discover each other and more often than not engage in amazing sex. Being in-love involves little to no work. As the spell of the romance program wanes, Stage 1, "Breaking Through the Family of Origin Blockade," begins. Stage 1 is all practice and work involving the resolution of each other's differences and family of origin stuff. Once differences are accepted and blocks from the past are resolved in a good enough way (see chapter 8), a couple can begin the work of learning repair mechanisms so that a potentially loaded behavior can be defused before it begins down the path of the self-generating Seven Deadly D's (see chapter 9). The end of Stage 1 is achieved when a couple has worked out a renewable contract for a satisfactory sex life. All of this is a transition to Stage 2, the "work" of achieving a high degree of independence for both partners. "Transition to Independence: Repair Mechanisms," involves finding ways to repair the damage caused by PRSD (including mending your sexual relationship). Stage 2, "The Realm of 'Me':

Independence as the Gateway to Interdependency," involves the full discovery of each partner's feelings of true selfhood. It is the world of "me and mine." Stage 3, "The Realm of 'Ours': Interdependence" is the discovery of the true world of "ours," the world of connection, commitment, and deep intimacy.

Chart 7B: Six Fundamental Problems Inherent in All Relationships

1. The Difference Between Being:

In-love (attraction and infatuation) and in-love and lust

Love (secure attachment, attunement, caring connection, presence, and intimacy), understanding love as energetic work involving stages of commitment and maturation

2. Differences

1. Gender
2. Temperament, tastes, idiosyncrasies, values, and needs
3. High-T (testosterone) and low-T people; discrepancies in sexual desire
4. Family rules—overt and covert
   a. Ethnicity
   b. Religion
   c. Money
   d. Parenting
   e. Householder—how the house should be kept
   f. Vocational

g. Sexual

h. Educational

i. Celebrational—how to celebrate birthday, holidays, etc.

j. Political

3. **Nonpathological and Pathological Wounds**

1. The normal biased world

2. Attachment trauma

3. Abuse and neglect

4. Developmental dependency need deficits

4. **Degree of Solid Selfhood**

1. Ego strength and "true self" actualization

2. Internal and external differentiation

3. Developing semipermeable boundaries

4. Level of emotional literacy

5. **Communication Issues**

6. **Familiarity (the Frozen Image) and Fate**

1. The terrible "dailiness"

2. Projection

3. Disaster (misfortune)

4. Betrayal

5. Familiarity

We've already dealt with number 1, the false beliefs surrounding our understanding of the romance program. Most researchers see being in-love as a *nonworking prelude* to love, not love itself. I've discussed how the "love molecule" dramatically raises each person's sexual drive (testosterone level) and how in twelve to eighteen months, people more or less go back to their normal testosterone levels. The heightened state of the in-love stage is nature's way of ensuring that we meet, mate, and reproduce, so that life will go on. It "did not evolve to help us maintain a stable, enduring partnership," as Helen Fisher wrote.

For the individuals who are or were in-love, the diminishment of the romance program can be an enormous jolt. It must be understood that the post-infatuation period, with its possible PRSD, is the end of the prelude to love and the *beginning* of the first stage toward experiencing real grown-up love. If you look at Chart 7C, I've outlined what I (and many others) believe are the three self-generating stages of maturing love, which begin when the in-love/lust stage (romance program) ends.

I use variations on the word *dependency* because I express the developmental stages of childhood as a struggle that starts with being co-dependent (symbiotically bonded with our mothering sources). From that we move to counterdependency, as we find our earliest sense of self by separating from our mothering sources. This is a stage of oppositional bonding. Toddlers fight for their selfhood by having tantrums and saying "No!," and a pure self-boundary statement, "It's mine!" From the counterdependency struggle for separation and selfhood, in later childhood we begin to establish our unique independence. This is the adolescent's struggle, par excellence. Teenagers often fantasize that they live with an "imaginary audience" watching them. Teenagers make a "personal fable" starring themselves.

Chart 7C:

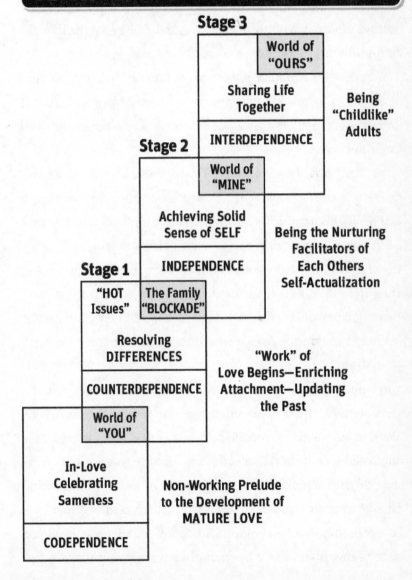

DEVELOPMENTAL STAGES OF MATURE LOVE

Stage 3

World of "OURS"

Sharing Life Together

INTERDEPENDENCE

Being "Childlike" Adults

Stage 2

World of "MINE"

Achieving Solid Sense of SELF

INDEPENDENCE

Being the Nurturing Facilitators of Each Others Self-Actualization

Stage 1

"HOT Issues" | The Family "BLOCKADE"

Resolving DIFFERENCES

COUNTERDEPENDENCE

"Work" of Love Begins—Enriching Attachment—Updating the Past

World of "YOU"

In-Love Celebrating Sameness

CODEPENDENCE

Non-Working Prelude to the Development of MATURE LOVE

They must make their lives unique and special. In late teenage years, high school, or the early years of college, we generally fall in-love and find ourselves ensconced in the mirroring eyes of our beloved. We find ourselves in a symbiotic bonding for the second time. Once our in-love trance ends, we begin the journey to mature interdependence.

I believe the romance program is the starting point of mature love. It is a wondrous time for most people, but to confuse it with mature love has, as we've seen, serious and potentially evil consequences.

In her book *The Anatomy of Love*, Helen Fisher discusses the length of marriage. For our ancestors, marriage seemed to last a very short time. In the animal kingdom, staying together for more than four years was unusual. This was enough time for the couples to have offspring and care for them. In four years, the offspring could fend for themselves. As marriage moved from being a political or social contract and merged with the in-love poetry and romance of the troubadours, it became a love affair.

As life expectancy grew beyond what ages had known in the past, we developed a new challenge—the long-term marriage. We still have scanty knowledge of how enduring marriage is supposed to unfold. We're slowly beginning to know what the long-term problems look like. My model of the three stages that emerge after the romance program ends is based on common-alities of highly functional and happily married couples that have been written about by therapists over the last seventy-five years. My stages also follow the childhood stages for developing a sense of identity—co-dependence, counterdependence, independence, and interdependence.

I advise the reader to remember that all the models therapists use are a product of their (usually highly) informed imagination. It is critical that models be created in order to deal with the many complexities of a marriage. The couples who never disagree or who communicate in a highly abrasive way *are* happy, although it is possible that they have such a low degree of selfhood that they have no idea what they are missing. The most important thing I'd ask of you is that you not terminate the relationship/marriage you are in; it may be a perfectly good enough love if you're willing to work on it.

8

Growing Up: Exorcising Your "Hauntings" by Repairing Your Wounded Inner Child's Developmental Dependency Need Deficits

Unless you finish your source relationships,
you'll never be in another relationship.

—G. I. Gurdjieff

The past is never dead. It's not even past.

—William Faulkner

The past is not a package one can lay away.

—Emily Dickinson

The recently deceased comedian George Carlin was once asked how old he was. He thought for a moment and then answered, "I'm one, two, three, four, five, six," and so on. What I got out of his joke was that he was saying that he could act in an age-regressed way at any given time. What George may or may not have known is that we are *most prone* to regress to stages where our developmental dependency needs have not been met, because we were abandoned, neglected, abused, traumatized, or enmeshed with a parent during the sensitive period when our brain was primed and ready to learn the age-appropriate developmental task it was supposed to learn.

Two good examples of this are the main dependency needs we had in infancy and toddlerhood. These are developmental needs that can only be fulfilled by depending on another. As adults our needs can be satisfied by *ourselves.* An infant lives in a world of "you," totally dependent on her mothering source for everything, but especially her narcissistic supplies. To get her narcissistic supplies, an infant needs to look into her mothering source's face and *see herself* mirrored there.

A child's earliest and most potent sense of self comes from her mothering sources emotional stability, presence, and mirroring face. This early mirroring is described as "a person's fundamental narcissistic supply." The infant cannot get this need met without *depending* on her mothering source. If she fails to get this need met in a good enough way, she moves on to toddlerhood with a developmental deficit. This deficit will be a real character defect, as the little girl will continually try to *get attention* and *be admired*, and that will be hard on her. Many of the people who do what I do—write books, lectures, do TV series—have (or had, if there's been some reparation) this narcissistic wound. Our work gives us admiration and applause most of the time.

DEVELOPMENTAL DEPENDENCY NEED DEFICITS (DDDS) ARE UNCONSCIOUS

It's important to say that developmental dependency need deficits are unconscious. We didn't know we had critical needs in childhood; we just had them. They were part of our survival. Nature provided us with an old brain that did not require thinking. The conscious brain (the neocortex) evolved later on. I'm trying to engage your conscious brain to examine your unconscious brain.

DEVELOPMENTAL STAGES ARE RELEVANT TO EVERYTHING (NEW JOB, NEW FRIEND, ETC.)

A toddler begins what many call "second" or "psychological birth." The "life force," mobilized by the innate affect of curiosity, moves the toddler to want to touch and explore everything.

He has an innate sense of self, wants to do things his way, and gains a sense of the power of autonomy by saying, "No," or, "I won't." Toddlers are also prone to temper tantrums and in late toddlerhood say, "It's *mine!*" These behaviors are quite bothersome to say the least, and they are among the dependency needs that are usually handled badly. They are basic developmental dependency needs and form the foundation for our core self-boundaries and sense of "true self." In order to grow up and learn to survive on his own, a child *needs* to separate. We must move from environmental support to self-support.

In late toddlerhood, a child wants to do things alone, but don't worry; he won't venture very far away. He is in a stage called oppositional bonding, which means what it says—he is separating, saying in effect, "I am me but I'm still extremely dependent and bonded with you." Because of a child's boundary setting, this period is called "counterdependency."

If a child gets these developmental needs met at the right time and without an excess of shaming punishments, he or she will not regress to those childhood stages later on. Then there is the flip side: during therapy sessions, I've heard many age-regressed spouses childishly fighting for attention and for what they thought was theirs in the marriage.

When childhood needs have not been met, they do not go away. Rather, they operate like "black holes" of energy, continually distorting whatever is going on in the present and sucking up energy as these needs clamor to be met. They will continue to exert energy until they are dealt with. When a person has serious developmental dependency need deficits (DDDs), they remain stuck at the developmental stage that has been unfulfilled.

Why all the discussion about dependency? People often confuse love with dependency. Counselors have to deal with this mix-up daily. It is most apparent in people who talk about suicide, who have actually attempted suicide, or who have become morbidly depressed because of unrequited love. They actually say, "I don't want to live without my spouse or lover."

Psychiatrist and author M. Scott Peck, in his amazing bestseller, *The Road Less Traveled*, describes how he responds to the statement, "I don't want to live without my spouse or lover." He tells the patient that he or she does not love his or her spouse (lover). "What you describe is parasitism, not love. Two people love each other only when they are quite capable of living without each other, but *choose* to live with each other."

We all have dependency needs. Distorted dependency is classified as a psychiatric disorder. It is called "passive dependent personality disorder." It is probably the most common of all emotional disorders. People with this disorder are so busy seeking to be loved that they have no energy left for love. They have a kind of inner emptiness crying out to be filled, but because their wounds create a bottomless pit, they never have a sense of completeness. Peck defines neurotic dependency as "the inability to experience wholeness or to function adequately without the certainty that one is being actively cared for by another" (pp. 98–99). In the early 1980s, this dependency disorder was written about extensively and was described as co-dependency.

Many books have been written on addiction in families. It has become clear that when one person is severely dependent (say an alcoholic or a food addict), the rest of the family, especially the spouse, becomes co-dependent. We had thirty-five years of learning about these extreme dependency disorders and how the family became addicted to the addict and the addict's drug of choice. Due to the pioneering work of Pia Mellody, Claudia Black, and Melody Beatty, we learned that in a family, there is no addict without a co-dependent, a co-addict. Both are stuck in a neurotic relationship or marriage.

FAMILY SYSTEMS

The psychiatrist Murray Bowen developed a *systems theory* of family function and dysfunction (which I've presented in my book *Bradshaw On: The Family*). Bowen found that the most critical aspect of any person's functioning health was what he called "differentiation" (a solid sense of self). A family's primary job is to allow all its members to differentiate, to become the independent persons they were meant to be. All of us have a true uniqueness, whatever it is that makes me, me and you, you. Parents with several children will tell you that each child has his or her own uniqueness. In fact, parents are often amazed at the unique interests and vocational direction that each of their children chooses.

SELF-SUPPORT VERSUS ENVIRONMENTAL SUPPORT

Fritz Perls, the founder of Gestalt therapy, described the goal of life as "moving from environmental support to self-support." We need to do this in order to be a self. Self-supporting means to be differentiated from one's family and making it on our own. To be differentiated, a person needs a valid sense of their own self, and this, more often than not, is somewhat different from their family of origin, especially their mother or father's projected expectations of them. Differentiation also presupposes that the stages of a growing person's developmental dependency needs have been satisfied in a good enough way. In the last few decades, especially working with alcohol and other addictions in families, it has become apparent that children will grow up undifferentiated, simply because their addicted and co-addicted parents, absorbed in their loveless addictions, could not be there to meet their children's developmental dependency needs. We describe these unfortunate youngsters as "adult children." They grow up, look adult, take on adult tasks, but can regress to the developmental stage where they get stuck at any time. Because of their *neediness*, rooted in their developmental dependency need deficits (DDDs), adult children are highly susceptible to frequent episodes of falling in and out of love and have a more than average propensity for addiction. When adult children marry, the result is often pretty messy. Without new awareness and repair work, PRSD will control their relationship.

Early on in his work, Bowen became aware that people tend to choose partners who are at or near each other's own level of differentiation (redneck sports addicts don't usually hang out with opera fans). In my work I saw one person after another choose someone as a lover who met their own unmet developmental dependency needs.

Psychologist Harville Hendrix found that most people choose a partner who is most like the source figure(s) who abused them in childhood. In short the "wounded inner child" in each of us searches for someone who looks like, acts like, or is like the parent who failed to meet our needs, or the source figure who abandoned, abused, neglected, or enmeshed us. When a chemical match is reached, two people are most likely to fall "in-love." Hendrix believes that we each carry an image that consists of our experiences with our source figures and forms what is referred to as a "love map." He called this brain-etched material your *imago*.

Nature abhors a vacuum. The child in us is still trying to get his or her needs met, and when "in-love" unconsciously believes he or she has found just the one who is most like the parent or source figure who failed them. Although our imago can move us toward a certain person, often we pick a partner who will wound us like our childhood abuser(s) did. A person chooses such a mate because being with them feels familiar. When two adult "wounded children" feel chemistry for each other, the match seems "perfect" —and during the infatuation period, it is perfect. The more wounded two people are before they find a chemical match and enter the romance period, the greater the intensity their being in-love will feel. But the greater the intensity of being in-love, the greater the PRSD will feel when the PEA dopamine cocktail wears off. And when it wears off, there will be two adult children at the same or near the same stage of neediness, without a clue as to what to do to create a mature, intimate love.

If you look at Chart 7C, you see that at Stage 1 of the developmental stage of love, there is a word in the upper right corner called "blockade," and by its side are the words "hot issues" from the first family. These hot issues are the DDDs each partner is carrying.

When I taught my family of origin class at Southern Methodist University, I used two very simple charts to outline a functional family and a dysfunctional family. In family systems theory, the chief component of the family is the *marriage*. As the marriage goes, so goes the family. As the functionality of each partner goes, so goes the marriage.

Carl Jung said it well: "The most damaging thing to the children in any family is the 'unlived lives of the parents.'" Jung had several things in mind when he spoke of the parents' unlived lives. But he most definitely had the parents' DDDs in mind. Where there is a part of Mom or Dad that is unfulfilled, that deficit represents a lacunae—a hole, as it were—that needs to be filled. A "needy" spouse will try to get his or her "needy" partner to take care of him or her; but since the partner is needy, too, the parents most often fight like two children, or turn to their children to fulfill their own neediness. In layman's terms, when one or both partners in a marriage have DDDs, their marriage will be "immature."

Look at Chart 8A.

Chart 8A:

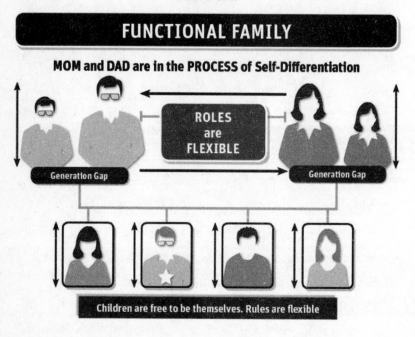

FUNCTIONAL FAMILY

MOM and DAD are in the PROCESS of Self-Differentiation

ROLES are FLEXIBLE

Generation Gap   Generation Gap

Children are free to be themselves. Rules are flexible

In this family, Mom and Dad are getting their needs met through their own resources, and through their loving relationship with each other. The parental relationship is the chief component in the family. Mom and Dad are in the process of being up-to-date with the developmental dependency needs of their inner child (i.e., they have grieved the loss of their earliest developmental dependency needs and are in the process of making them fully conscious and learning how to repair them).

MARRIAGE AS PSYCHOTHERAPY

One of the best things about getting married is that it gives couples an opportunity to heal their past. It also gives them a way to build their solid selfhood. Hendrix has pointed out that the marriage itself can be a form of psychotherapy. In the functional family, Mom and Dad are adults who have integrated their "wonder child," the source of their childlike fun, curiosity, resiliency, love of others, and a sense of humor. By healing the wounded child, the wonder child becomes available. True maturity incorporates all the traits of the inner child of the past. A healthy adult acts in a "childlike" rather than "childish" manner.

The children also help Mom and Dad repair their DDDs, because as each child goes through his or her own developmental stages, it activates that same stage that the parents went through. This gives both parents a chance to deal with whatever may be unresolved in themselves.

Having a *strong generational gap* is most significant, as it allows the children to be children and keeps them from being enmeshed in their parents' marriage. It prohibits the formulation of triangles that emerge when the parents are stuck in conflict and use one of their children to take the heat off the issues they are struggling with. Mom may become absorbed in her daughter's tap-dancing career, or Dad can become totally occupied with his son's baseball prowess. Each partner can avoid the other by being absorbed with their child or children.

In the functional family there are no rigid, absolute rules, and roles have a high degree of flexibility. Dad may be the breadwinner and do some of the household chores (vice versa, if Mom is the breadwinner), whereas in a dysfunctional family, it's just the opposite; the roles are either rigid or chaotic.

THE VERTICAL LINES

In the functional family, the vertical line symbolizes Dad's and Mom's personal "work" to get his or her own needs met. Their inner kids are standing outside of them, indicating each partner's conscious awareness of his or her past wounds and the presence of his or her "wonder child." Their wounds are no longer unconscious. I've drawn three lines between the parents. The two outer lines indicate that Mom can be vulnerable to Dad, and Dad to Mom. The inner line shows that each has a strong boundary for their privacy.

Each spouse is willing to be vulnerable to their partner. Each partner is willing to be rigorously honest about their own self. At the same time they have a boundary that allows each of them to have the privacy that is necessary for their personal freedom and growth.

THE GENERATION GAP

The generation gap between Mom and Dad's relationship and that of the children is absolutely crucial. Mom and Dad

Chart 8B:

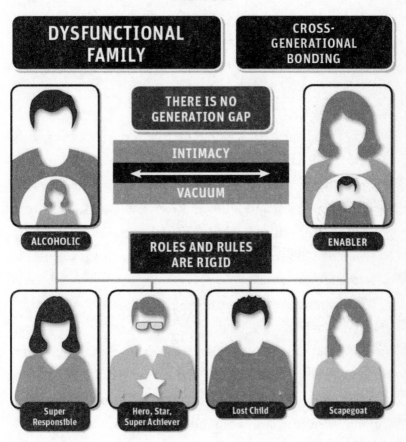

need a life apart from their children, a life that will hopefully be growing after the children have grown up and left home. In *Hope Springs*, Arnold and Kay failed to build their relationship so that when their children grew up and left home, they had nothing going for *their* lives. They were like two ships passing in the night. I think that it is almost "sacred" for Mom and Dad to have a night out every week, or as often as they can afford it. Their relationship is the *chief* component of the family. It should be kept strong and growing. Living for the children is a mark of parents fearing to deepen their intimacy.

PAMPERED CHILDREN

There has been a great failure in recent years that amounts to putting the children first and the marriage second to last. It should be the other way around. When the children see and experience a loving and intimate Mom and Dad, they have a good model for intimacy. Such a model helps them know how to be intimate, and offers them ways to handle things when their own love molecule wears off.

There are many families that are healthy, and many children who are being blessed by their parents' maturing love and intimacy. But more than half of the marriages in this country are not making it, and 17 percent of those couples who do stay together are living in an unhappy way. A majority of the children of dysfunctional families will act out these terribly troubled family problems.

If you look at Chart 8B—once again my attempt to make some complicated matters very, very simple—you can see this in the way I draw a dysfunctional family. In Chart 8A the children are free to be children. Evolutionary theorists tell us that one of the reasons we have the longest childhoods of all living beings is that children should be free to be children and take the time to prepare for a responsible adult life. They should have the time to explore the world around them and to experience the joys of childhood, playing, having playmates, and curiously exploring their environment. Playing is work for children, a kind of rehearsal for adult life. When parents are getting their *own needs* fulfilled through their own resources and through each other, they are not in a state of neediness—that is, they do not need their children to take care of their DDDs. The children *can depend* on their parents to get their *own needs* met. In Chart 8B, you have "needy" parents. A needy parent sucks the very life out of their spouse, and their needy spouse has nothing to give back. Needy parents suck the life out of their child, and the child has no way to know what is happening.

In Chart 8C the family is frozen around the father's alcoholism. Everyone is in a rigid role. It is governed by *no-talk, no-listen, no-feel* rules. Two children are enmeshed in their parent's marriage and trapped in cross-generational bonding. The daughter is her father's surrogate spouse. The son is his mother's surrogate spouse. The parents turn to their children to resolve their marital conflicts.

In Chart 8B I've put the figures of each parent's inner child inside of them as a way to indicate they have unresolved developmental dependency needs and are adult children. In Chart 8C, the father of this family was abandoned by his own father. Besides being an alcoholic, the father pours most of his attention onto his daughter. She is his Baby Doll. It is clear to anyone that this father (husband) cares more about his daughter than he does his wife. She (the daughter) forms a triangle that keeps

Chart 8C:

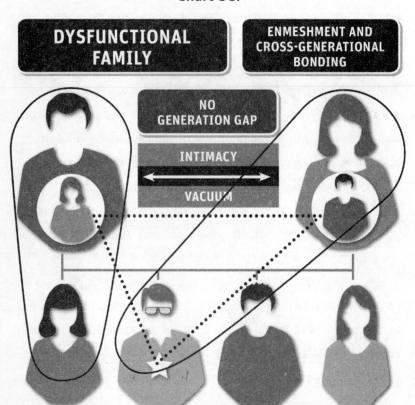

Dad from dealing with the issues he has with his wife. Basically, his neglected inner child thought that his wife would mother him in a way that his own mother never did.

His wife has made her middle son (her oldest boy) her surrogate spouse. The son is quite a star in baseball and football, and is the salutatorian in his class. Mom confides in this son, sucking him into her marital problems (including how disgusting sex is with his father).

The third child is withdrawn, indifferent, and failing in school. He is extremely needy; his parents are enmeshed with her older sister and brother. A third child's birth order job is to take care of the marriage. In this family setup, the third child is overwhelmed. The fourth child is also failing in school and is a real troublemaker. She's been in numerous fights at school and has been caught stealing several times. She is the family scapegoat. In fact, the only times Mom and Dad have any serious contact is when they are dealing with the scapegoat child.

In summation, I must reiterate how important it is that the first thing the couple who head up the dysfunctional family must do is deal with their own unresolved family of origin needs. In the later years of my marriage counseling, I would spend no time on the (most often childish) fights the couple would bring to counseling. The key was to quickly get at what I labeled the "hot issues" from each person's family of origin. In Chart 8C, the father had unresolved grief over his own father's abandonment of him. He was ravished with toxic shame, the feeling that he was flawed and defective. This was his father's shame. When a parent is an offender, they act shamelessly, and their victim has to carry their shame. Until this father felt some self-value, he was in no position to love anyone. He rejected those who did love him.

The mother in this family had fallen madly in-love with the father and had gotten pregnant at eighteen. Her strict religious family cast great shame on her and coerced her to get married. After she married she went into PRSD. She soon had children.

As her PRSD worsened, she turned to her gifted son out of her neediness. While it felt like he was special, the son was being sucked into a dysfunctional marriage and being deprived of his childhood. The mother in our dysfunctional family had never been securely bonded to her own mother (an untreated incest survivor) who was bedridden and sick all the time. The mother in the dysfunctional family felt too ashamed to ask for the love and nurturing she deserved. She had learned early on not to speak her own mind or to ask for anything. When she fell in-love with her husband, the wounded child in her adolescent body thought that her lover, her knight in shining armor, would love and care for her the way she craved. But once the PEA dopamine cocktail wore off, PRSD set in, and there was no one there but an angry and lonely little boy who had never grieved his own father's betrayal or separated from his alcoholic mother's entrapment. Both spouses were ravished by their own neediness.

I opened this chapter with Emily Dickinson's line, "The past is not a package one can lay away." I hope the meaning is clear to you now. For this marriage to work (and it surely can) each spouse must do repair work on their abuse issues and their developmental deficits. They must grieve their childhood wounds.

My book *Homecoming* takes a person from birth to young adulthood and shows them the process they need to go through to mend their DDDs. You could do the exercises in the book or attend a workshop on healing your inner child. Actually, going to a treatment center like The Meadows and doing the work with a therapist is best, but it must be with a therapist who has done his *own work* and can *let you grieve*. They must help you get to your repressed affects (feelings) and grieve the losses you incurred in early childhood. What is clear is that the first thing that each person must do is finish their own past and differentiate from their family of origin. If you're a religious person, there is a strong scripture that says, "I have not come to bring peace but a sword . . . I've come to put sons against fathers and daughters against mothers . . . and a man's foes will be those of his own household" (Matthew 10:34).

You cannot be an individual adult until you have physically and emotionally left home. The grief process allows a person to finish the past. It helps a person grow up. You have to say good-bye to childishness. The comedian Mort Sahl once said, "We would have broken up except for the children. Who were the children? Well, she and I were!" When two immature people find each other (essentially, two adult children) they are like two six-year-olds trying to create a household, have and raise children, and take care of the myriad responsibilities that go with building a family.

Not everyone may have serious family of origin issues. I hope you don't. But a lot of people do have these issues and often spend years in therapy *talking* about them but doing nothing to finish them. The hurts we carry from abandonment, neglect, abuse of all kinds, and enmeshment (being a parent's surrogate spouse) *have* to be grieved. This is the best way for them to be healed. Mending childhood wounds can take *two-plus years to heal* (there are many exceptions). This is why a treatment program like The Meadows can give you a real head start. The majority of our "quick-fix" culture does not want to spend this kind of time on healing their unresolved wounds from the past. Many have no idea of how they contaminate their present lives and exacerbate their PRSD.

Pia Mellody's book *The Intimacy Factor*, written with Lawrence S. Freundlich, offers people an outline of the "Feeling Reduction Workshop" (in the appendix on pp. 149–209), which she developed for The Meadows' treatment program. I do not recommend that a person try to do this work without a counselor or therapist. I have put warnings in my book *Homecoming* for a person to respect the work before trying to do it alone. I have had 350,000 people do my "inner child" workshop. We have a ratio of one therapist to every two groups of six; I have received more than a half million letters of thanks and reports of life changes (some dramatic) as a result of this work. It is a *very powerful* kind of work, so please don't trivialize it in any way!

THE QUADRINITY PROCESS

Another successful program for completing your past in a "good enough" way is called the Quadrinity Process. It was originally designed by Bob Hoffman as a result of his discussions with the psychiatrist Siegfried Fischer (you can read more about it in Hoffman's book *No One Is to Blame: Freedom from Compulsive Self-Defeating Behavior; The Discoveries of the Quadrinity*

Process). The whole process is done with *expert* supervision all over this country and in many parts of the world. The Quadrinity Process is a remarkable method, helping a person resolve their hurts and anger from the past and forgiving those who hurt them. Marion Pastor's book *Anger and Forgiveness: An Approach that Works* is a good summary of the process.

IMAGO RELATIONSHIP THERAPY

As mentioned earlier, Harville Hendrix created "Imago Relationship Therapy," which has been very successful in lessening marital pain. Hendrix and his wife, Dr. Helen Lakelly Hunt, founded the Institute for Imago Relationship Therapy, located in Dallas, Texas. A detailed outline of the therapy can be found in his book *Getting the Love You Want: A Guide for Couples* (a number one *New York Times* bestseller). The technique is based on the belief that we all carry an image engraved in our brains of all the source figures who raised us. We especially internalize a composition of the positive and negative traits of our parents (and any other source figures who were important in our lives). The image is mostly unconscious, but it guides us in selecting a mate. The imago partner is also unconsciously seen as the parent(s) who hurt us. The old brain, seeking self-preservation, moves us to work out the loss, conflicts, neglect, or abuse felt by being abused with the original parents. As mentioned earlier, nature abhors a vacuum—our unconscious energy is pushing for resolution.

In light of Fisher's findings, which we've been learning about throughout the book, this theory seems to embody a degree of imagination, as do all the theories of attraction. Nevertheless, the therapy based on Hendrix's theory (as well as some others), has proven to be very successful. I believe the love map or unconscious image of a desirable partner does move us toward one person rather than another, but without the biological life force (the DNA and HLA match), we have no chemistry with them. Imago therapy helps you heal your childhood wounds and traumatic abuse (if any). We *feel* chemistry for the person with whom we find a DNA match (DNA and HLA that is compatible but different than our own). This ensures our children's future by removing their chances of getting many diseases.

Imago therapy offers great help in dealing with the inevitable conflicts that will arise as Stage 1 of PRSD is ushered in (the clash of two different family systems each having its own overt and covert set of rules and rituals). If we have wounds from our childhood past, which most people do, we are attracted to someone who resembles the one—or a composite of those—who hurt, neglected, enmeshed, or abandoned us. Hendrix calls the stage after infatuation the *impasse.* I call it the family of origin "blockade." Hendrix has developed a very effective program to take couples through it. Working through Stage 1 of PRSD is absolutely essential for a solid connection and commitment. The imago program is an excellent guide for working through each partner's unresolved issues from the past. Imago therapy can help you "exorcize your hauntings" (the childhood wounds that will contaminate your marriage). This helps you integrate your *wonder child* by healing your "wounded" inner child (this process is clearly outlined in my book *Homecoming*). I'll end this chapter with a challenge from therapist Dr. James Hollis who writes, "Putting it crudely, only grownups can have effective relationships, and while there are people with big bodies and big roles in life, there are not many grownups" (*Why Good People Do Bad Things*, p. 104).

9

Stage 1: Breaking Through the Family of Origin Blockade— Learning How to Argue Effectively

The meaning of your communication is the response you are getting, no matter what you intended to say.

—Neuro-Linguistic Programming (NLP) Training

John Gottman, a leading researcher on the success and failure of love relationships, has written, "Some conflict and disagreement are crucial for a marriage's long-term success. Conflict is healing. In a sense, a marriage lives and dies by what you might loosely call its arguments—by how well disagreements and grievances are aired." One key to a successful and stable relationship is how well you argue, whether your style escalates tension or leads to a feeling of resolution. Learning a healthy disagreement style is crucial. It is not that complex or obtuse. You can easily learn a strategy for conflict resolution.

In Chart 7B, I outlined the various issues that I believe are involved in working toward mature love. The work of love assumes that a couple has their attachment program in place. It forms the basic foundation for the developmental stages I outlined in Chart 7C. All of us need a secure attachment figure. Our secure attachment figure represents our supportive emotional lifeline. I think this is why Gottman and others found some long-term marriages working rather well, although they seemed to go against everything that many therapists teach. These couples were bonded and had each other as a secure base. He and his colleagues found three categories of marital relationships.

AVOIDERS: THE NEVER DISAGREEABLES

Some couples simply agree never to disagree. They live with mostly loving and kind words toward each other. For those of us observing them, we think, "They've got to be kidding us; how in the hell do they resolve their inevitable differences?" The couples that I actually knew who appeared to agree never to disagree seemed to intuitively know when it was their turn to compromise or give in. I'm not talking about a relationship where one partner controls everything the other does so that there is never *any* argument. The couples I'm referring to seemed to have a sense of give and take, and know when to compromise. The few couples I saw in therapy who had agreed not to disagree came to me because of issues their children had. In one case, their child was being bullied at school. In another, their child was dyslexic. They had nothing ill or problematic to say about their marriage. I had some suspicion that the child being bullied had failed to learn any conflict resolution skills. Mom and Dad fired me before I could explore that issue—but they fired me very nicely!

THE CHRONIC ABRASIVES

I also know of couples who unashamedly argue a lot, and often in public. They seem to react to each other all the time. Their voices get loud and agitated, but they always seem to know how far to go, and they never go so far as to really shame each other. They are like George's parents on the television show *Seinfeld*. It's important to me that you know that such marriages exist and, according to Gottman, there are many others like them. I personally can't imagine being in either of these first two types of relationships, but once again, it works for them.

VALIDATORS

A third model, called validating, seems so clear and rational to me that I can't see how someone would not want to use it if they fully understood it. But that's not the way life is. So the model that follows is what I and many other counselors have come up with as an effective way to argue and resolve conflict in a nonshaming, proactive way that moves the relationship along. You can judge it for yourself.

YOUR LIFE BEFORE YOU FELL IN-LOVE

Once the PEA dopamine wears off, it is not just the testosterone levels that go back to normal. Many other aspects of each person's pre-romance life come back into play. The powerful chemicals that constituted being infatuated subside. The formerly cute, idiosyncratic things about your partner can become quite annoying, as in the examples I gave earlier. Male and female differences, while not as polarized as we've been made to believe, are certainly a factor to be dealt with. Many issues of noncompatibility, easily glossed over during the intensity of being in-love, start to emerge in the post-romantic stage. During the romance program, lovers rarely talk about political, religious, family, financial, or ethnic differences. Once the chemical bath subsides, these issues begin to surface. And perhaps the most potentially loaded issues are those that pertain to each person's family of origin (as shown in Chart 7B). In addition to the wounded kids trying to make their partner take care of their developmental dependency need deficits (DDDs), the "family rules," both overt and covert, are often the basic arena where arguments will arise in Stage 2 of PRSD. Family rules feel *familiar*, and we seldom thought about them as children. They become logged in our unconscious as the right way to do things. These rules will become more intense once a child is born.

My wife and I have one child together. As much as I thought we were in sync on most issues, it turns out we have some differences about the best way to raise our little girl. My textbook knowledge often clashes with her intuitive, commonsense mothering.

PREDICTING DIVORCE

My understanding is that John Gottman, working with fifty couples on two occasions, was able to predict with 90 percent accuracy which couples would be divorced within a given period of time (three years). To simplify what Gottman did to predict divorce, he basically paid attention to what people said about the beginning of their marriage and observed the ways the couples communicated. He presented what he calls "The Four Horsemen." Much like the biblical four horsemen of the apocalypse predict the end of the world, these behaviors can be the death knell for a relationship. They are the four stages of self-generating destructive communicating that could ultimately lead to separation and divorce if repair mechanisms were not used to stop their ever-increasing negativity. Look at Chart 9A. If the *criticism* of a partner's behaviors is not stopped, it will give birth to *contemptuous* and shaming judgments of the partner's very being. If that kind of judgment continues, the recipient can only view the partner as a grave threat, set up defenses, stop listening, and ultimately withdraw emotionally, and, if possible, physically.

Chart 9A: Self-Generating Cycles of Negativity that Destroy Relationships

The Four Horsemen:

Criticism: Judgment of partner's behavior as bad

Contempt: Judgment of partner's very being as bad

Defensiveness: Loss of listening, contact, and empathy

Withdrawal and Distance: Stonewalling, pouting, refusing to speak, and separating

As couples move down the stairs of degeneration, both partners begin to form an absolutized negative image of their marriage. Each feels like their spouse is the offender and that they are the victim. (I am a huge fan of Gottman and his wife, Dr. Julie Schwartz Gottman, and I recommend all of their work. I take full responsibility for any misinterpretation of the conclusions they have reached.)

THE SEVEN DEADLY D'S

Before I read Gottman, I had developed my own model for the stages of degeneration in a marriage. I called my model the Seven Deadly Ds (obviously copying the list of the Seven Deadly Sins). I actually enjoyed finding all the "D" words until I remembered how devastating and destructive my parents' divorce was for my brother, sister, and me. My model incorporates two of Silvan Tomkins's discoveries about the affect system: *dissmell* and *disgust*. These affects are experienced initially as bodily disdain (smell and taste) related to hunger. Smell is a far more important part of attraction than we have ever had empirical data to verify. As the self evolved, dissmell and disgust became more and more social safeguards. Dissmell is the core of prejudice, as well as any form of elitism. As a couple falls down the autodegenerative Seven Deadly Ds scale, they finally experience the withdrawal that follows the movement from experiencing an obnoxious smell and disgusting food, degenerating to dissmell, and often engaging in shaming each other for their hygiene. I most often experienced the descent into divorce as a fairly long process, immediately preceded by *dissmell* and *disgust*.

MY PARTNER'S SMELL

"I simply can't stand his smell. I don't want him near me," one spouse told me about her husband. Disgust seems to follow dissmell; it is the switch from "I want to eat her up" when you're in-love to "He makes me want to puke." When you're breaking up, dissmell and disgust occur slowly over a period of time, especially when no repairs are attempted. They virtually stop a couple's sex life. Dissmell and disgust are the sure marks of the bitter end of relationships. The psychiatrist Donald Nathanson writes, "I've never seen a marriage, a business partnership, or any relationship survive, once dissmell has entered the picture."

In my experience, the cycles of negativity are automatically degenerative unless some repair work is done. Doing nothing about your partner's denigration of you is doing something: making it worse. The autodegenerative Deadly Ds create a growing negativity that leads to *dissmell* and *disgust*, the *critical markers of impending divorce*. The stages of this destructive process must be interrupted if a marriage is to flourish and survive.

At the defensive and distancing stages, the marriage will stagnate and may end that way. Often during the first wave of PRSD, one or the other partner begins developing passive/aggressive anger toward the other partner. This may come out in destructive remarks denigrating their partner's behavior. If no stop action can be achieved, this kind of communication slowly intensifies and becomes demeaning and devaluing of the partner's very being.

This kind of communication is almost always shaming. Shaming forces a fight-or-flight response. Defensiveness and distancing slowly engenders dissmell and disgust. At this point, one or both partners develop an absolutized negative image of their partner and their marriage. Dissmell and disgust lead to a bodily repulsion of each other. The Deadly Ds occasionally run their course quickly. I remember counseling a young couple who were in dissmell and disgust when they came for their first visit. She spoke first saying, "I'm sure we could get closer if he learned how to use that disgusting thing of his." Of course she was referring to his penis, and she said this with her nose up in the air, her tongue against her front teeth, and her cheeks drawn tight.

He reactively said, "It's so big in there, I don't know which way to go. The smell is often disgusting." These remarks were said laughingly, but they were anything but funny; they were downright cruel. They were expressing disgust for each other's genitals on their opening visit with me. They lasted two more visits and never came back.

PESTILENCE AND FAMINE

I had other couples arrive for therapy acting like they were repulsed by each other. I call dissmell and disgust "pestilence and famine." They are the sure markers of the end of a relationship. Not all couples actually (legally) divorce at this point, but they definitely emotionally and sexually divorce. They are finished with each other and set up a nonverbal contract to avoid each other. This is a tragedy for any family. If there are children and they are living at home, they become acutely aware of their parents' dislike and contempt for each other, even though in public the parents put on the facade of a "happy couple." The children feel helpless to change it.

I've often asked each partner at this stage of their impending demise: "What was it that you loved and found magical about your partner when you were in-love?" A common answer is, "I was duped! I should've seen the handwriting on the wall." It's as if that mighty rush of tasty love chemicals had morphed into poison.

Chart 9B: The Seven Deadly D's

If you look at the following, you will see that there are healthy D's. They are:

Healthy D's:
• Disclosing your feelings • Declaring your desires • Discussing your dislikes • Divulging "shame secrets"
Declaring your desires or dislikes can easily lead to denigrating. **When any of the healthy D's lead to:**
• **Denigrating** attacks on your partner's behavior. The denigrating criticism must be stopped.
If not stopped, denigrating leads to:
• **Devaluing and demeaning** your partner's very being, which are viscious forms of shaming.
Shaming leads to:
• **Defensiveness** and the early formation of a negative image about your marriage. You begin to see your partner as an enemy. Seeing your partner as an enemy initiates chronic anxiety and causes reactive verbal conflicts.
You then seek:
• **Distance and detachment.** Either "wild" childish disputes or pouting and refusing to talk causes both partners to seek real distance and detachment.
Which, if not dealt with, leads to:

- **Dissmell**, which leads to isolation and dismissiveness. Dissmell is the core of all prejudices, gender, race supremacy, elitism, and discrimination.

  Which leads to:

- **Disgust:** The queasy feeling that makes one say, "She makes me want to vomit," the exact opposite of romance, "I want to eat her up." The whole marital relationship is now defined as doomed from the beginning.

- This results in **despair**, one or both partners feeling caught up in a game with no end. One or both feel like they are the victim and their partner is the repulsive offender. This most often leads to:

D   I   V   O   R   C   E

DEALING
WITH DIFFERENCES

Arguing and dealing with differences in an effective way is something I've had to learn. Everyone has some trouble communicating well. The great hypnotherapist Milton Erikson once said, "No one understands the same sentence the same way." Another quotation I like says, "If you're not getting what you want, try something else." This last statement puts the onus of responsibility on me, as it's so much easier to blame your partner or your children, employers, students, and so on, than take responsibility for what happened.

One of the exercises I use in my couple's workshop begins with a story:

EXERCISE

The Lumberjack and His Lady

(Just read the story and bypass any illogicality; just let the story have its emotional impact.)

It seems that Jack and Jill were still engaged when Jack's job called him to the deep, wild wilderness of Northern Canada. Jack was a lumberjack and had to go where the work was. The place he was called to was a little town called "Snake." To get in and out of Snake, you had to cross over a mile-long bridge that spanned a very wide river full of water snakes, crocs, and gigantic catfish. The current in the river was extremely dangerous, and many had drowned. Many others had just disappeared! The river was a little under a mile wide.

Jack and Jill found a nice little cabin and settled down. Everything went well for four months. They were so in-love and still having amazing sex, when a freak hurricane-like wind blew the bridge down. Jill was frantic as Jack would have to live in the lumberjack's barracks, and it would take ten months to rebuild the bridge. She could not survive alone for ten months.

Jill went to her friend, Joshua, who had a very small boat that he used for recreational fishing on special days when the winds were just right. Jill asked Joshua to take her across the river so that she could live in the lumberjack's camp with Jack. Joshua told her he was working on his post-romantic stress disorder. He said he had enough on his plate and needed to work on himself.

Jill was more anxious and fearful, so she went to the commercial fishing captain "Jawbone" Jeffrey. He was a known alcoholic and womanizer. He was Jill's last chance. She hadn't seen her fiancé in three and a half weeks. Jawbone told her that she would have to sleep with him and then he would take her across the river the next morning, weather permitting.

So she did the dastardly deed and, true to his word, Jawbone took her across the river and escorted her to the lumberjack camp. The reunion with Jack was a marvel to behold. They happily adapted to living in the wild. Things were going well, but Jill's conscience was tormenting her. She had been unfaithful in order to be with Jack. So, one night she confessed!

Jack blew up! He went berserk and kicked his beloved Jill out into the night. She was panicked and hysterical, cold, and almost naked when she ran into "Janzar" the Wild One. No one knew where Janzar came from, but he was clearly fed up with civilization. So he became a wild man and helped rescue people in the wilderness. When Jill found him, she told him what had happened. Janzar took Jill under his protection and went to the camp to find Jack. When he found him, he beat him up.

The story ends here, and I ask my workshop participants to rank the order of the characters in the story in descending order from the ones they liked the most to the ones they liked the least. I tell people to avoid philosophizing or moralizing and just let your gut take over. Then I ask people to share their lists with their partner.

Now, reader, take a few minutes and make your own list.

When I first did this exercise, my rank order was:

1. Joshua
2. Janzar
3. Jawbone
4. Jill
5. Jack

Now, I've been doing this exercise for forty years (with young couples, recovery couples, chemical engineers, CEOs of construction companies, and at the Baptist church, with little old ladies in their late seventies and early eighties). I've estimated that I've used it at least seven hundred times, and *never* has any one *not* been chosen! Every person has gotten a vote in the top three. A majority of the Baptist church ladies chose "Jawbone" Jeffrey! I told them I was a little surprised at that outcome. An eighty-seven-year-old got up and told me, "He told it like it was, Buster!"

The critical point about this exercise is the variety of answers and the variety of choices. I asked my groups if their rank orders reflected their personal experience. A majority answered yes. Those who voted for Jill (she always got the most votes for first) had had an experience of unrequited love or rejection.

I want people to know how different opinions and interruptions lack solid objectivity, and how with thousands of samples, there is a wide variety of differences. Differences are hugely subjective—couples need to know that. (We all need to know that.)

FERGUS AND IRENE:
MOVING FROM FEAR TO TRUST

The following is an account of my work with a very rigid client of mine, a doctor named Fergus, and his wife Irene. Our counseling led to a successful outcome for their presenting problem, and enabled them to learn a whole new way of having intimate communication.

Fergus was fifteen years older than Irene—he was sixty-one and she was forty-six—but he loved her vivacious personality and, as he told me, "her love of sex." They had been married for two and a half years when they came to me. Irene was an excellent tennis player and she had just started taking lessons from the new tennis pro, Todd, at Fergus's country club. She loved the guy's teaching skills and she invited him to dinner at their home. Todd was a muscular six foot four inches, quick-witted and classy. Fergus was threatened by him but felt that having him over for dinner gave him a chance to look him over. Fergus had to excuse himself about an hour after their meal ended, even though he knew that Irene and Todd were going to play gin rummy. He retired to his bedroom and fell asleep right away. He was awakened at 2:30 A.M. by the sound of Irene's laughter.

At our next session, Fergus expressed his anger at Irene, saying to her, "What the hell is wrong with you? You play rummy till the middle of the night! An older woman like you [even though she was hardly old] staying up with that woman-izing Todd?" I could see Irene move her upper body away from Fergus, and she refused to say anything about the situation. As Fergus continued to say critical things about Irene, losing total control and spouting hurtful things, I ended the session, requesting to see him alone.

TEACHING THE AWARENESS WHEEL

I spent a couple of sessions with Fergus. He was very angry at me for only seeing him and not Irene. I let him vent. I simply validated his distress and told him I thought and hoped he would soon understand. I then began to teach him what I call the Awareness Wheel (see Chart 9C), which has four parts: (1) Sensory data, (2) Interpretation, (3) Emotion, and (4) Volition. The Awareness Wheel has been a godsend for me and my wife, and a large number of my clients and workshop participants.

It became clear to me that Fergus was a man full of anxiety and fear. When he was sure I knew how distressed he was, he was ready to listen to me. I told him I was going to teach him a way to have effective communication with Irene. In our next session, I focused on the beginning of his upset. He said he *heard* his wife laughing and seemingly having fun at 2:30 in the morning. We discovered some free-floating anger over not having the luxury to stay up until the wee hours. He was a surgeon and had to retire early in order to get up at 4:30 each morning to get to the hospital. Fergus was highly skilled, in demand, and had a full load of operations for each of the four days per week he was in the operating room.

After some practice, I had Fergus use the Awareness Wheel. He said, "I woke up to the *sound* of your laughing. When I *looked* at the clock, it was 2:30 in the morning [that marked three hours of gin rummy]." We went on from the sensory data to the interpretation. In our original session that included Irene, he had originally accused her of being turned on by the young, virile, twenty-five-year-old tennis pro. As he ruminated over that, it led to the accusation of an affair, which he had absolutely no data to support. So I had him say to Irene, "I'm *imagining* you're turned on by Todd and are having an affair with him."

Our feelings flow from our interpretations (what we make up about the sensory data). So I helped Fergus realize that he felt angry because of what he made up, not for anything Irene had actually done! In reality, Irene liked Todd a lot, especially as her tennis coach. She was having fun experiencing him as a person by playing gin rummy. He had a great sense of humor. In general, Fergus was terrified that Irene would leave him for a younger man. I had him see that the feelings that came from his fantasy about Irene were made up by him. I had him practice saying, "I'm so afraid that you are going to leave me!" The last part of the Awareness Wheel is easy. Fergus needed to ask Irene what he wanted from her. Step 4 in the Awareness Wheel is about volition; it's about what you want to know or have your partner do.

When Fergus felt ready, we brought Irene back for a therapy session. I had them sit across from each other, making eye contact. When Fergus started expressing himself with the Awareness Wheel, I could sense that Irene wanted to really hear him. When he took responsibility for his fantasy, she moved closer to him, and when he expressed his fear and terror with tears that she was going to leave him, Irene got up and put her arms around Fergus. She was clearly moved by his honest vulnerability and wanted to be *close* to him—Irene spontaneously expressed her deep love for Fergus. She said she enjoyed Todd and thought she was making a lot of progress under his tutelage. Fergus had told her he wanted her to stop the lessons. Irene said she would not stop the lessons and instead invited Fergus to join her. Fergus agreed to take lessons from Todd, and that seemed to be the end of it. When Fergus was in the "critical parent" mode, dumping judgment and shame on his wife (the Deadly D of devaluing and demeaning), she moved physically and emotionally away from him. She stopped having sex with him. After our session, she moved toward him and held him. In later sessions, they told me they were having very fulfilling sex often enough.

FACTS VERSUS FANTASIES

The following is an exercise I use in every relationship workshop. It helps partners see how they project their own imaginations onto each other.

EXERCISE:

Facts vs. Imagine Using "I" Messages

Partners face each other. Each takes a turn and points out a *fact* about their partner (i.e., you're wearing a red shirt). Partners then take turns saying something they *imagine* about their partner. They do this three times. Joe starts out and says, "I see you are wearing a blue blouse." Sarah says, "I see you have a silver watch." Each does this, stating a fact, two more times. Then Joe says, "I *imagine* you're a pretty happy person." Then Sarah says, "I imagine you think this exercise is silly." Then they take turns two more times, stating something they imagine about their partner.

At this point, I have people stop and reflect on the three things they imagined about their partner. I tell them, "When you have your three imaginings clearly in mind, try each imagination on." For example, Joe would say "*I'm* a happy person and Sarah would say *I* think this exercise is silly." As they began the exercise, Joe was feeling exceptionally happy and Sarah did feel like the exercise was silly. Each came to realize that they projected their subjective feelings onto their partner. In most cases, one or all of the "imagines" can be owned by the person making them. In more technical terms, the things each person imagined are called "fantasy projections," usually fantasies coming from a person's *own* experience. The projection is not necessarily wrong, and when people know each other really well, the projections can be fairly accurate, but often they are not. With those we do not know well, they are just as often wrong. When they are wrong, they cause confusion and problems. Criticizing and blaming are generally wrong. When we do them, we're dumping our own stuff (often the disliked or disowned parts of ourselves) onto the other person.

If you look at Chart 9C, the Awareness Wheel, you can see that awareness begins with facts (or sensory data) and moves clockwise to interpretations (which are products of imagination or fantasy), since we cannot really know what's going on under our partner's skull and skin. Feelings follow our interpretations, and what we want from our partner comes next.

Chart 9C: The Awareness Wheel

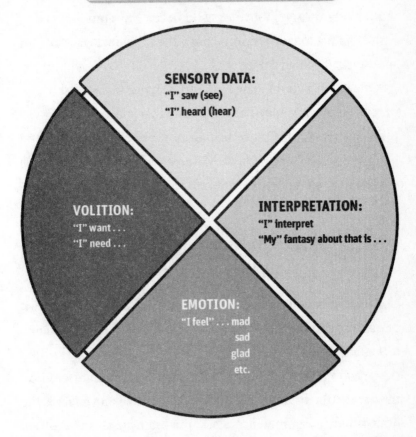

The most critical part of awareness is our interpretations. Every time we interpret our partner's communication, we are fantasizing—we are making something up. We use that exact language in our therapy work at The Meadows treatment center. We say, "I saw . . . or I heard . . . and what I'm making up about that is [whatever I imagine], and please note that since my fantasy is a projection, it could be coming from my unmet, unconscious need(s), my prejudices, my belief system about men, women, gays, lesbians, African Americans or my 'frozen images' about my spouse or whomever I'm communicating with." As marriages go on in time, the image we have of our spouse can become frozen.

Once I've made an interpretation, I have a *feeling* that it triggers. If I fantasize, imagine, or make up that you are happy, I will probably have the feeling of being happy or I could feel resentful because you are happy. On the Awareness Wheel, you also have volition—a willful desire or a want related to your spouse.

HOW DDDS CONTAMINATE THE AWARENESS WHEEL

Developmental dependency need deficits (DDDs) shut down one's ability to use the Awareness Wheel. They disturb and distort effective communication. DDDs, especially traumatic experiences, are frozen scenes from the past that are imprinted on the part of the brain called the amygdala. The amygdala is the brain's alarm signal, which alerts the brain whenever we have any fairly dramatic new experience—good or bad. I remember every detail about listening to a Notre Dame football game on the radio in 1943. Angelo Bertelli was the quarterback for the Fighting Irish who went on to win the Heisman trophy. I also remember the details of exactly where I was when President Franklin Delano Roosevelt died.

I also have vivid, painful memories of numerous scenes involving my father's alcoholic behavior. These evolved into issues of unresolved anger, loss of trust, and abandonment. When these traumatic scenes from the past remain unresolved, a present event that resembles even a single element from the scene can trigger the past anew. When that happens, a person's own awareness is overwhelmed by the repressed feelings and decisions involved in the out-of-date scene. Using myself as an example, instead of being in the present I become the young child of the past. I am now a grown-up man feeling the fear, anger, and distrust I did as a child. All my perceptions are distorted; I don't see what I see or hear what I hear. There's no way I can make a relevant interpretation of anyone else's behavior. My out-of-date feelings now rule my behavior and I cannot communicate in an effective manner, primarily because *I am not there*. Repressed feelings thus govern whatever interpretations I'm going to make.

After a few years together, when the chemicals that produce the Romance Program subside, people come out of their altered state of consciousness and are no longer in a swoon. They come back to either their normal self or fake self. Folks with normal selves that are reasonably up to date work through the PRSD and adjust to a life without chronic accelerated levels of dopamine; they settle down for the long haul. They have some challenging adjustments to make, but they have enough self-differentiation to make those adjustments in a good enough manner.

Those with false selves are in varying degrees of co-dependency. They will suffer with communication problems. I saw many men still enmeshed with their mothers. It's like they wear a pair of glasses with their mom's face printed on each lens. They do not really see their wife's face; they see her through the lens of their mother's face. Until such people do the grief work required to really leave their mothers (i.e., *really* leave home) they will re-enact the same issues they had with their mothers. I've been married twice, both times to very health-conscious women. Yet, I've seen my mother's hypochondriasis in both of them. My distortion and overreaction to their health suggestions are a result of my projecting my mother on them.

THE ANTIQUE STORE: USING SENSORY DATA TO MAKE A FANTASY REALITY

Suppose I'm in an antique store with you. You are my wife. I ask you to refrain from buying any more antiques. As we browse around, I *see* you talking to the store manager and I *hear* you say, "I'll call you tomorrow." With that sensory data, I interpret that you are going to buy an antique. As I make that fantasy, I *feel* angry, and when we leave the store I tell you what I saw and heard, what I'm interpreting, that I'm feeling angry, and I *want* to know what your intentions are. This is an actual incident I had with my wife in Ireland.

To argue well and deal with this conflict, it is important that I use the word "I" and that I express my fantasy and make my feelings and desires known. Using "I" lets my partner know *me*, that is, know what's going on inside of me. Using "I" avoids criticizing and shaming. Using the phrase "my fantasy" or "what I make up about that," makes the interpretation "mine" and it makes it clear that it is not an absolute—that it is not necessarily true. Expressing the feelings and desires also allows my partner to know what is going on inside of me. In fact, the argument is a way for us to know each other in a fuller way. This is why Virginia Satir stated that there could be no real intimacy without conflict and negotiation of differences—and why John Gottman sees effective arguments (ones that lead to greater awareness of each other) as part of a marriage's long-term success.

My use of the Awareness Wheel is a gross simplification of a book called *Alive and Aware* by Sherod Miller, Elam Nunnally, and Daniel Wackman. I highly recommend this book. By the way, my wife *was* going to buy an antique for *me*. Her mother had asked her to buy me an antique pen for my birthday! So what "I" made up was true, but I also made up that it was a willful desire of my wife to get something for herself, when, in fact, she was buying a birthday present for her mother to give me!

SENSORY-BASED DATA

There are two other instruments that can be of immense help in clarifying conflict and arguing effectively. Take a look at Chart 9D, entitled "Represented Reality." I created this as a rough epistemological chart to show why a genius like Milton Erikson would say, "There are no two people alike. No two people who understand the same sentence the same way." Epistemology is the study of the deep structure of language. An epistemologist wants to know *how* we know. I first presented Chart 9D in my book, *Healing the Shame That Binds You*.

Chart 9D:

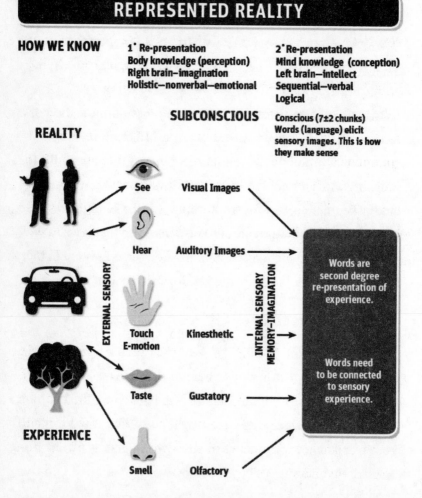

No one knows "reality" directly. Immanuel Kant showed us a few centuries ago in his book *The Critique of Pure Reason* that we do not know or experience things in themselves. What we know are our verbalizations and representations of experience. We use words to talk about what we believe happened, but they can never tell you *exactly* what happened. Words are like the maps of territories. A map is never a complete representation of a territory of which it is the model. People tell us what they consciously experienced, not what actually happened. In my chart, reality is in the left corner: the tree, car, and people. The middle part is the first degree of my re-presentation of reality: I see it, hear it, touch it, taste it, and smell it. Our first-degree representation of reality is our sensory-based data, and our best communication of reality is sensory based. In the example of the antique store, if I'd told my wife I was angry, and nothing more, she would have had no idea what the word "angry" meant, because words (like "angry") are second-degree representations.

ONE WORD, MANY INTERPRETATIONS

If I say the word "circus" to a group of people, everyone will go to their sensory- based representation of the word. Someone might see a tent, someone else might experience the taste of cotton candy, and someone else might hear circus music. While I use one single word, there can be various sensory representations of that word.

I remember being in a meeting where I saw my friend crying. I asked him what was wrong. He said that his dog had died! Frankly, that *made no sense* to me. I'd never had a dog and, since I'd been a paperboy and chased and nipped at by dogs, my main experience with them was negative. It's clear that if someone uses a word, the only way you can understand it (or have it make *sense*) is to go to your sensory-based representation of the experience that the word elicits. I'd had no positive experiences with dogs; therefore, I had no sensory experience of a beloved dog dying.

A year later, I bought my son a dog, which we named Culley. After a few weeks with us, when I came home the dog would jump up and get so excited he'd pee on himself. I had always wanted a friend like that! Not the urination, necessarily, but one who was overjoyed to see me and who loved me no matter what. When Culley died, I cried.

When we argue with each other, it is imperative that we translate words into sensory-based data. To learn to communicate and argue well we have to be cognizant of the fact that words must be translated into sensory experiences in order for them to make any sense to us.

Check out what a significant other says to you by asking questions: If a person says, "I don't like your brother," you might respond, "What specifically don't you like about him?" If the answer is, "He's too arrogant," ask, "How, specifically, is he arrogant?" If he or she says, "He hardly talked to me Sunday at your house," you can say, "How did that look and sound?"

If he or she answers, "I said, 'Hi Bob,'" and he started talking to someone else," you now have the *sensory data* that goes with the sentence "I don't like your brother."

Break words into sensory data. Instead of saying, "You are so kind," say, "I saw you help that homeless man get up; then I saw you give him some money, and I heard you encourage him. I felt warmth and love toward you." The most effective communication is sensory based. In my chart you can see that it is closest to *reality.*

The following model is a guideline for translating words (second-degree representations) into *being* language, which is concrete, specific, sensory-based data (first-degree representations). This model was created by the founders of Neuro-Linguistic Programming, Richard Bandler, Leslie Bandler, John Grinder, and Judith Delozier, a group of modelers who spent many years watching, listening, and videotaping three of the greatest communicators of our time: Fritz Perls, Milton Erickson, and Virginia Satir. What the neurolinguistic modelers discovered was that these three giants in the therapeutic field were constantly translating people's words and fantasies (things they made up) into concrete, sensory-based information. The sensory-based data was as close to reality as it was possible to get. This allowed the expert therapists to be absolutely clear on what their clients were saying. By using the model rigorously, they could go a long way in keeping their own fantasies and biased belief out of the communication.

In the following chart, "The Hard Data Translator Tool," don't be deterred by words like "Deletions," "Lack of Referential Index," and so on. Just *read* the examples and it will make good enough sense to you.

THE HARD DATA TRANSLATOR TOOL

The hard data translator tool (my name for it) was developed by John Grinder and Richard Bandler as a means to help increase the flow of information between human beings (see their book *Frogs into Princes*). The basic premise is that words are meaningful only in that they *anchor* some sensory representation in an individual. During the codification of sensory experience into words (as an individual speaks) and the process of decoding (as the individual listening to the speaker transforms the auditory stimulus into his or her own sensory representation), important information can be lost or distorted.

The hard data translator tool provides an identification of linguistic patterns that could become problematic in the course of communication and a series of responses that two individuals may use to ensure more complete communication. The hard data translator tool makes language concrete and specific. In so doing, *fuzzy data* words (second-degree representations) are made into *hard data*, that is, become concrete and specific. Each specification, completion, and clarification connects words with the concrete *experience* that they represent. Thus, the hard data translator tool translates words back into experience. More specifically, *it translates your spouse's words into your spouse's experience. It thereby keeps you from translating your spouse's words into your own experience* or distorting her words with projections from your own wounds.

Chart 9E: Hard Data Translator Tool

1. **Simple Deletion:** When some object, person or event (noun phrases or noun arguments) has been left out of the surface structure.

    Example: There are some things about our marriage that I'm uncomfortable about.

    Response: What specifically are you uncomfortable about in our marriage?

2. **Lack of Referential Index:** When an object or person (noun) that is being referred to is unspecific.

    Example: People in this family are lacking in good motivation.

    Response: Who specifically is lacking good motivation?

3. **Comparatives Deletion:** When a referent is elected during a comparison (i.e., good; better; best; more; less; most; least.)

    Example: It's better not to face that issue.

    Response: Better for whom? Compared to what?

4. **Unspecified Verbs:** Verbs which are not entirely explicit where sometimes the action needs to be made more specific.

Example: The new maid bothers me.

Response: How specifically does she bother you?

5. **Nominalizations**: When an ongoing process is represented as a static entity in a way that may distort its meaning.

   Example: Our marriage is in trouble.

   Response: What aspect of our marriage is in trouble?

6. **Presuppositions**: When something is implicitly assumed in the other person's communication that may, if taken for granted, cause limitations to a person's choices about the experience.

   Example: If you know how hard I've worked on our child's spelling, you'd probably just put your hat on and leave.

There are three presuppositions in this statement:

   1) You don't know;

   2) I've worked hard; and

   3) You will act a certain way.

Response:

   1) How do you know that I don't know?

   2) How specifically have you worked on it?

   3) How do you know what I would do?

7. **Model Operators of Possibility and Necessity:** Statements identifying rules about or limits to an individual's behavior.

   Example of Possibility: I'm so tired but I can't relax.

   Response: What stops you?

Example of Necessity: I shouldn't let anyone know how I feel about our Sunday school.

Response: What would happen if you did?

Semantic Ill-Formedness

8. **Cause-Effect:** When an individual makes a casual linkage between their experience or response to some outside stimuli that is not necessarily directly connected, or where the connection is not clear.

   Example: Your suggestions about improving our marriage confuse me.

   Response: How specifically do they confuse you.

9. **Mind Reading:** When an individual claims to know what an individual is thinking without having received any specific communications from the individual.

   Example: My husband never considers my feelings.

   Response: Why do you think your husband never considers your feelings? Are you saying your husband has never once considered your feelings?

Please use this chart, based on the Meta Model developed by Bandler and Grinder. It will help you immensely, I promise you. Read their book *Frogs into Princes*. It will give you a full, rich discussion of this model and how to change fuzzy data, or second-degree representations, into hard data (i.e., concrete-specific, sensory-based data), or first-degree representations.

10

Transitioning to Independence—Repair Mechanisms in General

Enriching and/or Salvaging Your Sex Life in Particular

In the meantime
There are bills to be paid, machines to keep in repair,
Irregular verbs to learn, the Time Being to redeem
From Insignificance.

—W. H. Auden

Docility is a major trait of healthy shame and maturity. We all have an endless amount of things to learn about intimacy, especially if we've had poor models to look at. Putting the issue of discrepancy of sexual desire aside for a moment, one of the major resources each person needs in overcoming the denigrating and devaluing stages of negative dissent is, for lack of a better phrase, "a tool kit of repair mechanisms."

My model of the Seven Deadly Ds suggests that if no repair work is done, the stages are autodegenerative. The key phrase here: *if left completely alone* are autodegenerative. One stage will spin automatically into another, starting the decoupling, and then unraveling the relationship. The Seven Deadly Ds have to be interrupted—and the sooner the better. If we don't find a way to intervene and interrupt an emerging pattern of criticism, it will escalate and become demeaning, shaming, and degrading.

SUGGESTED REPAIR INTERVENTIONS

The following lists are some suggestions for repairs. No one thing works all of the time. *Flexibility* is a great strength to have when working on repair mechanisms. One inflexible rule is getting rid of rage. I was a "rage addict" and had to get help for it. I was on the verge of losing all the love from my ex-wife and our children. If you rage at your spouse and family, I promise you that you need outside help; otherwise, it will ruin your life. I recommend that you read John Lee's book *The Anger Solution*. What I've found so valuable in Lee's work is his understanding of regression and how to uncover it. What he calls the "Detour Method" is a simple way to track down age-regressed material and the anger (rage) that goes with it. Childhood developmental deficits are losses. To grieve them you need to get at the *anger* that is part of the grief process. The anger is yours and should not be spewed onto others.

REPAIR MECHANISMS

1. Use "I" messages and avoid "you" messages—which are mostly judgmental.

2. Listen empathetically, and validate what you hear. Repeat the content as well as the nonverbal affect of your partner's communication. Mirror your partner's affect and offer sensory-based data as feedback, such as: "I saw your lips tremble"; "I heard your voice tone soften"; "I experienced you as sad." (Don't give advice about why he or she is sad.)

3. Focus on one thing at a time, known as gatekeeping. "You were late for dinner tonight," instead of, "You are late for everything we do!"

4. Edit yourself. Omit words that have nasty overtones and focus on the data at hand. For example, say, "You are late," instead of, "You no-good bastard!"

5. Tell your partner what you *can* and *want* to do rather than what you *can't* and *won't* do. Instead of saying, "You never want to go on vacation with me," say "I want to go on a

vacation with you." (Give sensory data, for example: "I liked sitting by the beach together and just talking when we were in Hawaii two summers ago.")

6. Offer positive appreciation wherever possible. Make it concrete and sensory based. Instead of, "You are a great mom," you might say, "I saw you help Ariel pick up her toys. You seemed to know how tired she was, and I loved your nurturing care."

7. Practice small, easy-to-do, cherishing behaviors for limited periods of time, say four times a week. This is especially good if the cycle of negativity is intensifying. A cherishing behavior is one you know your partner likes, such as a phone call during the day to say, "I love you." If your partner is the breadwinner and you are not, give him an agreed upon time to decompress when he or she gets home from work. If you both work, take turns having the agreed upon time.

8. Schedule discussions. Set specific limits for discussions, especially if they involve topics (issues) that have caused trouble in the past, or it is late at night.

9. Soothe your partner, either physically or emotionally. Touch your partner, even a small gesture, such as holding their hand or just placing your hand on their arm. It has sometimes worked for me to ask for a hug before giving each other feedback. Of course, this is no good if your partner is very angry or upset.

10. Use humor. Humor can defuse a tense situation. Over the years, you probably have shared jokes or humorous

anecdotes. They may be about in-laws or some experience you had together. Or you may say something related to current events—"At least I am more conscious than the mayor of Toronto," or, "It could be worse; you could be married to: Herkemer [someone you know they dislike]." Humor can be a pattern disruption—although it could aggravate your partner, so work carefully with it.

11. Practice "feeling" probes. Ask the other person what he or she is feeling and then listen nondefensively.

12. Employ metacommunication. This is a complex-sounding term that simply means you discuss in advance how you intend to communicate, and that what you're about to say is not meant to be malicious.

13. Call a "stop action" if flooding is imminent. Gottman recommends that couples measure their own resting pulse rate. Actually know your base pulse rate, and if it increases 10 percent or more during a discussion, which causes flooding, call a stop action. It usually takes twenty minutes to recover. Take a walk, do breathing exercises, meditate, or reschedule the discussion for tomorrow. (Stop action is a repair mechanism the Gottmans recommend. I like it a lot, but I found that my patients would not use it effectively in their early repair work. Several highly reactive clients told me that I was "crazy" to think that stop action would work. Those who started with less stressful repair mechanisms gradually used stop action quite effectively.)

MAKING YOUR PARTNER CHANGE

Cybernetics teaches that the part of a system that is most flexible will usually be the most effective and has the greatest possibility of controlling the system. In therapy, it is said over and over again that you cannot change your spouse. Partners continually try to do that. They argue about the same things over and over again. This kind of arguing is ultimately what's fruitless and leads to boring and repetitious fighting called "the game without end." I gave an example of Cindy and Robert earlier in the book. Each person's behavior creates the other's behaviors. This kind of arguing will not carry the couple's intimacy forward; it retards it. Each one is hell-bent on changing their partner and keeps using behaviors that keep their partner the same. A therapeutic slogan that has emerged from "systems thinking" about dysfunctionality says, "The more they try to change, the more they stay the same."

There is a way to change your partner. It is based on a simple rule that I've already stated: "If what you are doing does not work, try something else." You don't have to be a nuclear physicist to grasp that one.

CREATIVE INTERVENTIONS AND CHANGE

A woman I'll call Irma Lee came to me for counseling, complaining that her husband was thirty minutes to an hour late for dinner about three days a week. It obviously bothered her a lot, so I asked her what she had done about that. She said she called him a "selfish, no-good bastard." I asked her how long this tardy behavior had been going on. She answered, "Oh, about fifteen *years*!" I asked if she had done anything other than call him a selfish, no-good bastard. She answered, "No." At this point you don't need any therapeutic training to tell her that her name-calling doesn't work! I suggested that she *do* something quite different, that is, that she change her response to his tardiness. She and I talked about her options. I am quite taken with the work of Dr. Milton Erikson, a hypnotherapist who is known for his unusual interventions in therapy. I modified one of his strategies on "pattern interruption" to help Irma Lee find solutions.

I suggested that she wear her pink leotards with a red tail on any evening she suspected that her husband would be late. She had told me about this outfit in an earlier session. She had worn it to an all-girls' overnight party where the ladies were asked to dress crazily. She asked me if I was serious and wanted to know why I suggested this. I asked her to trust me and just do it. So she reluctantly accepted my recommendation that she wear her pink leotards with the red tail when greeting her husband.

Three weeks later, I had my next counseling session with Irma Lee. She was quite happy when I saw her. She said her husband interrogated her for a while the first time he came home late and found her dressed in her leotards with the red tail. Since that evening, for the first time in a decade and a half, he was not late, even once! My fantasy is that he thought she was flipping out—going nuts—and wanted to get home to watch over her.

Creative interventions like the one I'm describing don't always work—nothing works all the time—but they can cause a real pattern interruption, and can change behaviors that are in a rut. The critical point is that if you want to change your partner, you can, if you're willing to change your *own* behavior first. In other words, if I want to change you, I have to change me, and the change in my behavior needs to go on for at least three months. At the end of that time, if you've failed to get what you want, try something else.

I've found that one of the best ways to defuse criticism is to respond with a little-used word out of context. To the criticism, "You left the garage door open again," you respond with, "I know, the traffic was so otiose tonight."

Your critic will have to think about the meaning of the word otiose, and what that has to do with traffic. It confuses the critic and forms a pattern interruption, which slows down the momentum of the criticism. It works a lot of the time.

WHERE YOU KNOW YOUR PARTNER WILL NOT CHANGE

There may be a point, after you've made seven clear personal changes for three months at a time, that there is still no change in your partner. At that point, you have to choose whether you're willing to stay in your relationship and accept that your partner is *not going to change* and look at your options for enhancing your quality of life. After a couple of years of your changing with no helpful response from your spouse, it is possibly a time to seriously consider divorce.

I've discussed a second principle, which also puts the onus of responsibility on oneself: "The meaning of your communication is the response you're getting no matter what you intend."

THE "HOW" OF A POEM

At one time I taught a class on English poetry at the University of St. Thomas. One day I examined a few of Robert Frost's poems using a book entitled *How Does a Poem Mean?* The "how" of the poem illustrates the way the poet puts the sentences and sounds together to tell the tale. While I found my lesson fascinating, a large number of my supposedly top honors college freshman did not share my enthusiasm. On a little exam I gave, 85 percent failed! Initially, I was angry, and ruminated over these students' laziness. I went on and on until it dawned on me that maybe (just maybe) I had not done such a good job in teaching the "how" of the poem. It is a switch to examine the "how" rather than the "what" of a poem. I finally became sure that I had not taught it well. Instead of blaming the students, I took responsibility for a poor job of teaching and took a different approach and got a good enough response.

When we place the responsibility of interacting on the way we are behaving, we have *some* control over doing something about it. If we change the way we are behaving we can get a different result. The more you have a solid sense of self, the easier it is to take personal responsibility for outcomes you don't like.

THE DISCREPANCY OF SEXUAL DESIRE

I mentioned that the most dramatic effect of the waning of the romance program is the reduction of testosterone levels. The chemicals that saturate the brain during the infatuation period are dramatic in their elevation of testosterone. Whatever the base level of testosterone is at the beginning of the in-love romance program, they are *drastically* elevated during the time we are in-love. No one seems to know for sure how long the testosterone brain saturation lasts, but the new discoveries by Fisher found seventeen months to be the average time span, and, as I mentioned in Chapter 2, there seems to be a high level of agreement among other researchers that the in-love period lasts from twelve to eighteen months. I have found it can go on much longer for the partner who experienced rejection or who never married their beloved. Once the chemical waves subside, the desire for sex subsides. It is fairly well known that the frequency of sex subsides considerably over the years of a marriage. Couples married longer than ten years tend to place a higher value on admiring and respecting each other, having a friendship with their partner, and making them their secure base.

WHEN YOUR FIRST CHILD ARRIVES

John and Julie Gottman conducted a long-term study of 130 newlywed couples. At the end of their study, they concluded, "The new data shocked us. Two thirds of the new parents self-reported that they were very unhappy after the birth of their first child" (Quoted by John Gartner, "Childolatry," in *Psychology Today,* Sept. 2014).

Both partner's testosterone (but more OFTEN in the female) diminishes after having a baby, and this is intensified with more than one child. Once again, nature is interested in procreating and increasing complexity. However, when a high-T spouse has courted a low-T spouse, the PRSD can be quite impactful, especially if nothing is done to create a solution. And while it seems like the high-T partner is hurt the most, the low-T person feels rejection as the time of sexual withdrawal is extended. In Part I, when Paul used the word "fine" in response to Shirley's "let's just cuddle," it didn't mean "everything's okay." Instead, it was a call to anger and the need for revenge. And remember how Sandra said she would never initiate sex again after Colby's Madonna anorexia (MD) seizure?

NO MAGICAL SOLUTION

Frankly, I've not found anyone who has the magic key to the problem of the discrepancy of sexual desire. Many write a good game, but the longitudinal studies of their success are nowhere to be found. I'm more optimistic about the success of sexual therapy than most. Dr. Pat Carnes is a pioneer in the field, and we have a highly effective treatment program at The Meadows. If the family of origin differences and the developmental dependency wounds are not dealt with effectively (in a good enough manner), the sexual issues may escalate. And if couples reach the stage where they are redefining their initial attraction to each other, the counselor begins to hear things like, "I don't think I was ever really attracted to Hank [or whomever]," "I think I was immature and lonely," or, "I was going through an experimental phase."

I agree with Dr. Nathanson that if couples have reached a high level of dissmell and disgust, they have varying degrees of *revulsion* for each other. I've never been involved with any couple who worked through that. I spent many counseling sessions looking at in-love behaviors (especially the behaviors rooted in the elevated testosterone that became manifest in the amazing sex stage). I've already suggested that it would be fairly abnormal if either spouse felt like they did when first in-love all the time. The few couples I counseled who had a rigorous sex life (sex at least once or twice a day after they'd been married for a couple of years), were extremely immature—their marriages didn't last. I do not intend for this to be an absolute statement! It is limited to my experience.

ROMANCE REVISITED

Memory is selective, and in the later stages of a marriage there is usually a degree of real memory loss concerning the sexual intensity of the early days of infatuation. Still, in dealing with disorder of sexual desire, it will help couples if they can focus on what they *do* remember about the first months of the infatuation stage: remembering when they first saw each other and how their feelings of being in-love developed; having each partner use concrete, sensory-based descriptions.

Loving behaviors are an integral part of the romance program. In the beginning, lovers are playful, laugh a lot, and shower each other with strokes (physical and emotional signs of appreciation). There is a lot of hugging, kissing, and gentle touching in the early stages of being in-love. Hugging and spontaneous kisses are cherishing behaviors. Cuddling at night without any expectation can lead to more than cuddling. Couples in-love work together and help each other solve problems. They make their partner's needs a priority. The great psychiatrist Harry Stack Sullivan defined love as the state where my beloved's needs and security are as important as my own. A criterion of true love is when one cares as much about his partner's anxiety as he does about his own.

In working with couples, I found it useful to point out the obvious shared experiences they had. Although one couple in particular that I worked with continuously squabbled with each other, their shared focus was their offspring. They had a slow-learning child, and both partners had spent a lot of time together looking for ways to help her learn faster. They also agreed on special times to share with the child in an effort to enhance her self-esteem.

The early in-love behaviors are especially important for the males, who more often have a higher baseline testosterone level. In her questionnaire, Fisher found that women are more turned on by gestures of love: love letters, poetry, and acts of tenderness. For the high-T male with a low-T partner, doing those earlier in-love behaviors or doing them for the very first time can be a powerful stimulant for initiating lovemaking. I found it very helpful for couples to understand what was happening as the PEA dopamine wore off, so that the high-T partner would not take diminished desire as rejection or the end of love.

TALK ABOUT YOUR SEX LIFE

It's crucial to discuss sex. Talking about rituals that turned you on may help, like having sex in a darkened room, keeping silent while having sex, "talking dirty," or telling your partner in detail what turns you on sexually. For others, there may be special rituals that form templates of arousal. I remember one woman telling her husband in concrete detail what turned her on.

As strange as certain sexual desires seem, we all have unique templates of arousal. Our partners are not mind readers—in this, or any other form of communication—and cannot know exactly what turns us on unless we describe it or actually show them. In a counseling session with one couple, the wife told her husband, in step-by-step, graphic detail, *exactly* what she liked and wanted. She left *nothing* to the imagination, starting with how she liked to be kissed, the intensity of the kisses, and the duration. It turned into an erotic road map of exactly where he needed to go on her body, and what she wanted him to do once he got there. She even told him precisely how long he needed to stay in each area, and then told him how she would reciprocate while on this superhighway of pleasure. She was definitely a woman who didn't mince words, and her reward for sharing so openly was a vibrant and energetic sex life with her husband.

Just like doing a presentation for work, sometimes visual aids are helpful in getting your point across. One of my clients used a dildo to show his wife exactly how to perform oral sex on him. Their sex life was revitalized as a result.

While at first you might feel uncomfortable talking about your wants and needs, in time you may feel safe enough to demonstrate exactly the way you like things done. Think of it like having an itchy spot on your back. If you wanted someone to scratch your itch, you would tell them what needed scratching and have them experiment until they found the exact spot. In this case, it's your G spot!

MADONNA ANOREXIA

For those who identify with Madonna anorexia—the message in your head that says you "don't have sex with someone you love and cherish"—you have to willfully remove the "dirty" fantasies about strangers and sensitively replace them with erotic fantasies about your spouse. It takes time, but it will help a great deal. I have helped several people with Madonna anorexia by changing their fantasy life and by doing some anxiety-reducing exercises.

One of my clients had been shamed within a matriarchal household. Consequently, he loved to imagine he was the slave of raunchy older women. He had a fixation on their buttocks, and his fantasies revolved around them demanding he pleasure them in this one specific zone. He truly loved his wife, but because of his childhood issues, he connected carnal pleasures with shameful fantasies. I needed to help him see that healthy sexuality is important in a relationship, and that with a few changes in perspective, he could rework the fantasies to help him have an exciting sex life with his wife. I helped him imagine gently holding his spouse's ample derriere. I suggested he think of her buttocks as a cushion to lay his head on, and to connect that with her kind and nurturing femininity. It seemed a bit corny at the time, and might sound strange, but it worked! It was important for him to focus on his wife's sweetness and nurturing and to then view her as a whole person, to connect sexual pleasure with her as another human being—not disincarnated buttocks.

BILL AND SUE REVISITED

When Bill and Sue, the couple I discussed in Chapter 4, hit the wall sexually with their PRSD, I spent a few sessions helping them to understand what was happening to their sex life, especially the PRSD over the low-T's sexual withdrawal. I further helped them understand some of the conclusions that have been discovered in studies of long-term marriages. As the years go on and your children arrive, both of you will have diminished sexual desires. Both parents' testosterone levels diminish as you raise a child or have children. And when the child or children become the major focus, "more than a hundred studies show that marital satisfaction falls off a cliff after the birth of the first child and doesn't do much better until their last child leaves for college" (John Gartner, "Childolatry," in *Psychology Today*). After years of empirical study, John Gottman concluded that "most unhappy marriages seem to flounder on the same rocks: children."

At first, Bill was not particularly receptive to any of this information. He wanted the amazing sex they had experienced during courtship. He accused Sue of using him sexually so that he would marry her. After their first child was born, Bill's sexual desire did subside a lot. After their second child, I convinced Bill and Sue to work on some exercises to help rekindle their sexual flames. I can't tell you that I always got couples to do touching and holding exercises—but those who did, like Bill and Sue, put aside their pride, realizing that holding on to it was not worth losing each other and their new family.

Bill had that overmasculinized fear of vulnerability. I found that same fear in the majority of my male clients. Men are taught as boys to shelve their feelings, especially their sadness. They are conditioned to keep a stiff upper lip and never show any vulnerability. This inevitably leads to the overmasculinized false self. The most important thing I got Bill and Sue to do was to have special times each week devoted solely to each other. These times have to be concrete and specific—for example, a late supper on Wednesday evening and a Saturday afternoon brunch. The children need to know that these are times their parents are alone.

FAVORITE IN-LOVE BEHAVIORS

I instructed Bill and Sue to each make a short list of their favorite in-love behaviors, the ones that had been especially valuable in their lovemaking earlier on. I gave them good information on the chemicals vasopressin and oxytocin, which enhance touching and the desire to be close to each other. I had them make a commitment contract to begin taking action to improve their sex life.

LESS ECSTASY—"STILL GOOD"

Bill and Sue's sex life became far less spontaneous and ecstatic than in the romance period, but by being willing to stay in sexual contact, the powerful chemicals vasopressin and oxytocin eased their awkwardness. Vasopressin and oxytocin, two closely related hormones made largely in the hypothalamus and the gonads, produce many of the behaviors associated with attachment. Vasopressin is nature's chemical for attachment. Vasopressin seems to be the chemical that causes male mammals to feel the paternal instinct.

Oxytocin is also made in the hypothalamus, as well as the testes and ovaries. Oxytocin is released in all female mammals during the birthing process. Scientists have shown that oxytocin stimulates bonding between a mother and her infant, as well as the feeling of adult male-female attachment. Both vasopressin abnd oxytocin are secreted in sexual intercourse during stimulation of the genitals and during orgasm. Oxytocin is especially powerful because it sensitizes the skin to touch and causes a tranquil and calm feeling. Oxytocin also has an amnesic effect, blocking negative memories (at least for a while).

After their initial PRSD, it took Bill and Sue a while before they enjoyed having regular sex again, and their sex life has had its highs and lows, which is not unexpected. I saw them off and on for about eleven years. At our last visit, they were both satisfied with their sex life.

ORAL SEX

In my early childhood and adolescence oral sex was very much a secret. In my mother's generation of women it was frowned on and considered disgusting. Remember the reaction Kay had about oral sex in the movie *Hope Springs*? Today is has become more and more acceptable. And in today's generation of young lovers it seems to be commonplace.

Over the years I had females who sought counseling concerning oral sex. They had experienced cunnilingus for the first time with their new lovers and they loved it but felt dirty. Others came to me because they felt either shame or guilt for enjoying fellatio. Many had swallowed their lover's seminal fluid and although it has aroused them to orgasm, they felt they were dirty.

As part of one's template of sexual arousal, oral sex is perfectly natural. When we love we want to be incorporated with our beloved; we want to be one with them, and satisfying them sexually helps fill this desire.

I counseled many couples who keep their sex life alive with oral sex. They found that pleasing each other manually and/or orally was less threatening. Other couples, like Kay and Arnold in the movie *Hope Springs*, had never engaged in it, although Arnold certainly wanted to. I found that holding, touching, and kissing exercises actually led to oral sex for some marital partners.

Oral sex can service romantic feelings. In a personal communication with Helen Fisher, psychologist Gordon Gallup of the University of New York at Albany stated that his research indicates that oral sex in general and seminal fluid in particular can contribute to romantic passion. He and his collaborators report that the fluid that surrounds sperm contains dopamine and norepinephrine as well as tyrosine, an amino acid the brain needs in order to manufacture further dopamine (*Why We Love,* p. 195). Male ejaculate also contains testosterone, various estrogens, oxytocin, and vasopressin, all of which contribute to feelings of romance. The various estrogens in semen aid feminine arousal and orgasm.

Seminal Fluid and Depression

Gordon Gallup and his research students, Rebecca Burch and Steven Platek, submitted a paper to the *Archives of Sexual Behavior* 13(26), 289–293, which asked the question: "Does semen have anti-depressant properties?" They suggest several ways seminal fluid might be an antidepressant for women. Seminal fluid contains beta-endorphins, substances that can reach the brain directly and calm the mind and the body. Male seminal fluid contains the essential ingredients for all three of the basic mating drives we have discussed in this book. The feeling of romance and the Romance Program are the result of intensified energy and passionate action. These elements certainly cannot coexist in a depressed person (*Why We Love,* p. 196).

I discuss oral sex in order to demythologize it. In the Victorian era, sex outside of wedlock was considered dirty, but we have evolved beyond that. The same can be said for oral sex, which was also once considered depraved behavior. We are sexual beings, and I hope this discussion helps you to explore this facet of pleasing your partner in your sex life.

DON'T LOSE TOUCH— SEX IS GOOD FOR YOU

What's important is that couples not withdraw or refuse to talk about the problem, and even more important, that they continue to have sex. Having sex helps create attachment. It helps if the low-T partner can think of *sex as a gift of loving care*, because during orgasm, vasopressin dramatically increases in men and levels of oxytocin increases in women. It is for these reasons vasopressin and oxytocin are also called the "cuddle chemicals." They contribute to the fusion, closeness, and attachment between a man and woman. Keeping the act of sexual intercourse alive is important for your relationship. *Sex is good for you.* It helps keep your skin, muscles, and bodily tissue in tone. It offers excitement, and oxytocin and vasopressin can (not always) increase testosterone, which is the fuel of romance and sexual desire.

Another reason couples need to keep their sexual love going is that it enhances and stimulates their attachment to each other and can also renew some of the primordial romantic energy. This is absolutely imperative because without some excitement and euphoria, the boredom or the "terrible dailiness" brings out the perceived negative traits of both partners.

CHANGE THE "NO-TALK" RULE

It's crucial that you talk about your sex life. If not, those who are high in testosterone will tend to whine, nag, and criticize. That will in turn drive the low-testosterone partner further away. Then you have the bitch and nag/silence cycle I talked about earlier.

The will as a "physical force" is the principle I talked about earlier, and it's crucial to be aware of this: You have to act yourself into a right way of feeling rather than try to feel yourself into a right way of acting. The low-T person won't feel like having sex, but if two partners talk about it and have a reasonable time, contract to act sexual, the low-T partner will often find the sex enjoyable. The "cuddle chemical" will be released, and you'll feel closer together.

THE DEVIATED SEPTUM REVISITED

The "deviated septum" is the way Kay and Arnold's therapist described the state of their marriage in the movie *Hope Springs*. At its height, folks with deviated septums have a hard time breathing. When the autodegenerative stages reach this point, the couple's marriage is doomed to arrive at dissmell and disgust, which amount to an almost animal rejection of each other. The only thing that first moved Arnold to action in the movie *Hope Springs* was the therapist telling him that Kay would probably divorce him when they returned home. Arnold needed to take swift action.

When marriages have reached the low point of third-degree PRSD, couples must act themselves out of it—quickly. It might be difficult to do this without the help of a therapist, as they usually can't or won't work out their "stuckness" by themselves. That pattern of their core dysfunction may be completely unconscious at this stage. Many are completely unaware that desire, in general, and sexual desire, in particular, are integrally related to their solid sense of self. The couples I worked with who were experiencing high-level disorder of desire had very little desire for *anything*. They had little ambition and had settled into a vapid and somewhat boring existence, showing very little desire in any aspect of their lives, including sex.

While Arnold and Kay did not seem to get any good results with their therapist in *Hope Springs*, the exercises they did attempt to complete had the impact of changing their brains. It took Kay's strong move to leave (to get a divorce) to trigger their renewed sex life. The "action principle" is most important in renewing a couple's sexual behavior.

11

Stage 2: The Realm of "Me" — Independence as the Gateway to Interdependency

Love your neighbor as yourself.

—Mark 12:31

*A solid sense of self is arguably humankind's
most unique evolutionary achievement.*

—Dr. David Schnarch

I n her immensely helpful book *The Dance of Intimacy*, Harriet Lerner writes, "Changing any relationship problem rests directly on our ability to work on bringing more of a self to that relationship. Without a clear, whole and separate 'I,' relationships do become overly intense, overly distant, or alternate between the two." Earlier, in Chapter 7, I stated that the family's basic job is to allow all its members to differentiate, to become the people they want to be and discover their own unique calling and destiny.

KNOW THYSELF,
IN GREEK MYTHOLOGY

In Greek mythology, the Delphic oracle told those who presented problems to "know thyself," which seemed like a mysterious answer. In fact, this simple instruction is a tall order and one that cannot be done alone. Finding ourselves is a whole developmental process. It begins in our mother or primary source figure's mirroring face. It continues throughout our childhood and reaches what the great psychologist Erik Erikson called our "identity crisis" in late adolescence and early adulthood. It continues as we fall "in-love," become attached, and attempt to create a mature love relationship. Knowing who we really are is the way to stop burdening others with our unresolved issues.

In *Finding Meaning in the Second Half of Life*, Dr. James Hollis writes, "What we do not know about ourselves nearly always proves a terrible burden on others" (p. 111). What I believe Hollis has in mind are our developmental dependency need deficits, our unresolved grief (wounds), and our shadow (the unconscious, disowned parts of ourselves that we project onto others).

DANGERS OF BEING A "FALSE SELF"

Not truly knowing yourself is disastrous when it comes to falling in-love. A person in the throes of love is temporarily incapable of reflecting on their own inner self and sorting through the projections that are keeping them in their entranced state. Furthermore, when we are in-love, our *projections* depersonalize the other, whom we profess to love. When one has no real sense of self, or is full of self-hate and toxic shame, they may try to love over and over again, but the subject of their love becomes an objectified projection of their own emptiness, and their lovers become artifacts of the psyche. Developing a healthy sense of self is the embodiment of nature's plan for us.

THE SELF AND THE TRUE SELF

We cannot really love without a solid sense of self. Two of the great psychiatrists of the late twentieth century, Harry Stack Sullivan and M. Scott Peck (both deceased), offered a definition of love that involved selfhood. Peck defines love as "the will (the choice) to extend *myself* for the sake of my own and another's spiritual growth." Sullivan felt that love exists when my beloved's feelings, needs, and desires are as important to me as my own. A person has to have a solid sense of self to love the way Peck and Sullivan describe love.

WHAT IS A "TRUE SELF"?

Every spiritual tradition has taught that we have a unique, unrepeatable self. Most spiritual traditions call our true self our soul, a part of us that our ancestors considered immutable. Many people don't like words like *soul*, so I like to present serious scientific works that posits the existence of a unique true self that every person is born with. I like to turn to a recent work in evolutionary psychology entitled *The Adaptive Design of the Human Psyche*, by Malcolm Slavin and Daniel Kriegman, who state, "We have, from the very beginning, some form of implicit intuitive capacity to know certain givens about ourselves. We have a class of motivations that are largely independent of the shaping and regulating influence of the relational world. We could never be designed in a way that permits the claim that 'motivations arise solely from lived experience.'"

Slavin and Kriegman underscore our intuitive capacity to know our true self. They believe our true self is negotiated and renegotiated throughout our lives. They write, "The true self follows from our intuitive capacity to be *alone* in the presence of others . . . and to intuitively know certain givens about ourselves." In another place they argue that the true self can be experienced by noting your "sense of vitality, who and what brings you alive, and where you fit within a relational context."

FREUD AND REPRESSION

Slavin and Kriegman believe that what Freud referred to as repression is most closely related to our "true self." We repress the true self until it is safe for us to own it. James Hillman has written a book called *The Soul's Code* in which he shows how one famous person after another repressed their true self in childhood but then it flourished in adulthood. Admiral Perry, who discovered the North Pole, was an absolute sissy who rarely left his mother's side.

The Spanish bullfighter Manolete was timid, fearful, delicate, and sickly until he was eleven years old. When he moved into his twelfth year, everything changed, and he became obsessed with bullfighting, which he began to do in his late teens. He distinguished himself by changing the old styles and renewed the ideals of the corrida (the bullfighting system) and courageously faced the thousand-pound black bulls with razor-sharpened horns thundering toward him. At age thirty, he lost his life to one of those bulls, named Islero, when the animal gored him through the groin and belly. This once-timid child, who might've faded into obscurity, became a national hero and had "the largest funeral ever witnessed in Spain" (*The Soul's Code*, p. 211).

Perhaps the best example is Oprah Winfrey, who was born into poverty and had a difficult childhood. She was first raised by her grandmother in Mississippi, then by her mother in Milwaukee, and finally by her father in Tennessee. She suffered sexual abuse by three different men, starting when she was only nine years old, and lived in fear and trembling. She sought solace in books and learning but ran away from home as a teenager to escape the abuse. Frustrated, her mother sent her to live with her father in Nashville. He was strict but encouraging, making her education a priority. She graduated high school and got a job in broadcasting. At first she struggled with her career, floundering as a news anchor and hard-news reporter—she was thought to be too emotional. But she finally found her niche as a talk-show host. That choice made it safe for her true self to emerge, and this once-poor girl who wore dresses made out of burlap sacks became one of the wealthiest, most influential, and most recognized women in the world.

THE UNIQUE

We must have independence and a solid sense of self-esteem or we cannot possibly love or give ourselves to the one we love. How can I love you with all my heart if I don't know who I am? My solid sense of self-differentiation is my core reason for being. Being *me* is the fulfillment of my calling and destiny. Being me implies that I know who I am and that I have a fairly sure sense of what I'm doing here. The Jesuit poet Gerard Manley Hopkins expressed this beautifully in a stanza of his poem "As Kingfishers Catch Fire." He wrote:

EACH MORTAL THING DOES ONE THING AND THE SAME:
DEALS OUT THAT BEING INDOORS EACH ONE DWELLS;
SELVES—GOES ITSELF; *MYSELF* IT SPEAKS AND SPELLS,
CRYING *WHAT I DO IS ME: FOR THAT I CAME.*
(EMPHASIS IN ORIGINAL)

Lovers must work through all their trite and trivial childishness to help each other actualize each other's true selfhood.

ACT AS IF—IMAGO DEI

The great spiritual masters argued that God, in his omnipotence, is far too immense for any of his creatures to be a manifestation of anything but an aspect of their maker. They argued that each of us is a special nuance, a special incarnation of our Creator. Think of someone you truly love. If you had to use one word or phrase to describe them what would it be? For my son, John, I'd choose "objective and honest." For my wife, Karen, I'd choose, "faithful and empathetic." For my daughter, Ariel, I'd choose "independent and curious." For my stepdaughter, Brenda, I'd choose "courageous and determined," and for my stepson, Brad, I'd choose "eccentric and creative." I could go on and on. I hope my point is clear. Obvious traits manifest their owner's uniqueness. They are also traits that your Higher Power must possess. By knowing and loving my son, wife, daughter, and stepchildren, I can have an immediate sense of their Creator's essence.

SACRED LOVING

Hence, by knowing and loving each other, we can get a glimpse of the Divine—a glimpse that only you and only I can show forth. So by my knowing and loving you, I can know and love some aspect of Divinity that you alone manifest. You are the *only book* in the library that can reveal a special glimmer of the Divine, and when you die, that book is gone forever. Thus, if we can create a mature love together, we can transcend nature and enrich our spirituality. The "unique incarnation theory" is a belief. It is utterly unprovable. I'm not trying to impose it on you. But suppose it were true. What an incredible thing to live in a world of sacredness. Imagine each spouse seeing their partner as a scared revelation, as an incarnation of God. I offered my clients who were in Stage 2 in the development of their mature love the opportunity to live *as if* this theological position were true. In certain cases, I gave it as an assignment and told them to live as if this theory were true for ninety days. For a minority, it just didn't work. But for a large number of those who practiced this belief, the results were beyond my expectations!

When the great Jewish theologian Martin Buber focused on the "I and Thou" relationship, he had a special sacredness in mind. I and thou *help each other to fully actualize the true uniqueness of each other*, and in that uniqueness, they help actualize God the Creator. Our whole life is a journey of becoming the one and only incarnation that can reveal a nuance of the godhead that we alone embody, and that cannot be known in any other way. All of creation, especially the highest levels of love, are part of a magnificent revelation that sends chills down our spine as we glimpse what Divine life and love must be like. Couples, therefore, are here for each other. Each is to be the "guardian of the other's solitude," as Rilke said. For true love, we are also to be the facilitators of each other's discovery, of what the poet David Whyte called, "the water of your *belonging*" (my emphasis). What exactly is the water of your belonging?

Rilke wrote a poem called "The Swan." In it, he described how awkward swans are when they walk on land. Out of the water, they are awkward, out of the element of their calling and purpose. Once the swans find the water, they move effortlessly as if they were being carried by a whirlpool of grace. They become, Rilke says, "more like a king, more like a queen." After reading this poem, the poet David Whyte asks us, "Where is the water of your belonging? Where are the places in your life where you are the most graceful? Who are the people who bring you alive?"

Remember that Slavin and Kriegman called your true self the place of vitality, aliveness, and the place where you seem to fit. When you find that behavior, that place, and those people, you will have begun to find the place of your calling and destiny. Surely one of the great acts of love is helping each other find our water of belonging. Each will be the facilitator of the other; each will be each other's helpmate.

The larger purpose of romance and lust was to achieve a true connection and attachment with one other human being.

Hopefully you had a "secure attachment" to your mothering source. Your new attachment can heal you if you were poorly attached.

RECIPROCAL LOVE AND SUPPORT

How could I know that in supporting my wife's artwork and her wonderful projects, I was moving into a quite transcendent place? I realized that I could go beyond myself (I had a self to go beyond!). Likewise, out of her love, she praised my work, participated in my workshops, and led me to a fuller recognition that I was doing far more than helping people give up their truncated fantasies and childish blocks. I was giving them hope, helping them to enter their journey of self-discovery, and be an active navigator of the long journey home!

In a couple's growing love, especially in Stages 2 and 3, they move into a territory that they really didn't know was there. But they could've never gotten there without their arguments and childish fussing and scorekeeping during the early years. As Dr. Scott Peck says, "our conflicts call forth our courage and ingenuity." In many ways, our conflicts *create* our courage and our integrity.

MIRRORING

As an infant you learned about yourself through your source figures' mirroring eyes. In Stage 2 you learn about yourself through the nurturing eyes of your beloved and the eyes of your true friends. I've seen a lot of friendships between spouses in Stage 2.

Fortunately, by Stage 2 married couples have a realization of where they've been and know what is worth letting go of and what seems to be worth keeping because it's full of energy and relevance to our true selves. They also know what problems will never be fully resolved. The arrival at Stage 2 brings each partner a kind of raw wisdom. The Serenity Prayer used by AA members says, "God grant me the serenity to accept the things I cannot change, the courage to change the things I can, and the wisdom to know the difference." Wisdom is about knowing your actual strengths and knowing your limits. Wisdom gives us the greatest gift of loving someone. We can have the gift of a very different vision; *we can see our partner's otherness as otherness.* We see them in their "realm of me." This realm of "me" began in toddlerhood as they began to separate and form the foundation of their personal ego boundaries. Saying "No," "I won't," and thunderingly declaring "That's *mine!*" is someone's first statements of selfhood. Each of us had the courage to leave our comfort zone and let the life force move us to separate from others and search for our true self. Failure to meet these first fragile attempts at boundaries mean that they will recur later in circumstances that make them more disruptive and damaging in our adult life.

Fortunately, these regressed emotional blocks can be worked on, and each partner can reach a point where they give up their childish stuff. They can become an adult with a solid sense of self. Being an adult means giving up childishness and living with childlikeness. Having a solid sense of self also means having good, semipermeable boundaries.

BOUNDARIES

Good fences make good neighbors.

—Robert Frost

My dear friend Jack Soll, a brilliant therapist in Los Angeles, shared with me a lot of what follows. Boundaries are like the borders of a country. We need passports to go from one country to the next. Boundaries are like doors that only we can open. Working on our developmental dependency need deficits help us develop good boundaries.

Developmental dependency needs include:

1. The right to have a space of your own.
2. The right to decide who can touch you and where you can touch them.
3. The right to decide when, how, and in what way you want to be sexual.
4. The right to neutrality of emotions; they are neither right nor wrong but are just the way you feel.
5. The right to your own ideas and opinions (you simply have to take the consequences of your thoughts).
6. The right to choose your own Higher Power and to worship as you please.

There are many other factors that constitute a person's solid sense of self-differentiation (independence). Without boundaries, no one can have a solid sense of self. Some boundaries are specifically gender oriented. For instance, males want and need a space of their own (it doesn't have to be a cave!), and while many women have strong and special needs for alone time, generally women like togetherness. Women know how to contain their emotions and generally like to share them. Women are not as afraid of vulnerability as men are (of course, there are always exceptions to the rule).

AN EXERCISE TO MEASURE YOUR SENSE OF SELF-DIFFERENTIATION

Our capacity to deceive ourselves is great. We need to check out our solid sense of self from time to time. Chart 11A is a test to measure your solid sense of self-differentiation. It is not intended to be all embracing, but it can give you a sense of the simple issues involved in self-differentiation and offer areas that you may need to work on. Each of these ten statements involves ego boundaries. A low score is an indicator that you need to put some energy into the particular issue in question. After you assign a number—4, 3, 2, 1, and so on—relative to each statement, add up the total. If your final number is 18 or less, you have some work to do.

Chart 11A: A Test to Measure Your
Sense of Solid Self

Assign the appropriate numbers to the following sentences based on your experience:

1. Always true: 4

2. Often true: 3

3. Seldom true: 2

4. Never true: 1

_____ 1. I know what I feel and express my feelings, especially anger, when it is appropriate to do so.

_____ 2. I know what my needs and values are, and I stand firm when they are threatened.

_____ 3. I have a balanced picture of my strengths and weaknesses (vulnerabilities) and present that picture to my significant others.

_____ 4. I address difficult and painful issues and take a position on matters that are important to me.

_____ 5. I state my differences with others and allow others to do the same.

_____ 6. I stay emotionally connected to significant others even when things get intense.

_____ 7. I know how to calm myself when I'm experiencing anxiety and fear.

_____ 8. I enjoy solitude (being alone with myself) without isolating (withdrawing from others).

_____ 9. I know my place in the universe. I have chosen a Higher Power to love, honor, and respect.

_____ 10. I accept the suffering that comes my way and engage it as an opportunity to grow.

Nature's need is to have us find a lover, get attached to them, and build a family. But the need for love goes far beyond the romance program. Mature love requires the willingness to give. As we grow in-love, we come to care about our partner as we care about ourselves.

12

Stage 3: The Realm of "Ours"— Interdependence

. . . So we grow together,
Like to a double cherry, seeming parted,
But yet a union in partition;
Two lovely berries molded on one stem;
So, with two seeming bodies, but one heart;

—*A Midsummer Night's Dream, 3.2.208–12*

Take a look at the last square in Chart 7C, "Interdependence." I like to compare this last stage to "two people playing the same song, but with different musical instruments." They each have their *own* skill (he plays the piano and she plays the violin). When they play together, they create the song. The song is not his or hers, it's theirs. It is a shared creation.

THE AGED RABBI

In 1796, the elderly rabbi Menachem Mendel Morgensztern of Kotzk said, "If I am I because I am I, and you are you because you are you, then I am and you are. But if I am I, because you are you, and you are you because I am I, then I am not and you are not." I've quoted that statement in four of my books. The rabbi clearly understood that a *relationship can't have interdependence unless the two people have independence*. Each whole person loves the other as a whole person. There is holiness in this "I and thou" kind of loving union. Because each partner is a whole person, they are not "needy." They have needs, but they don't need the other to *make* them whole. Each has their own life, which they share with each other. They have spaces in their togetherness, as the poet Kahlil Gibran says, because each has a solid sense of self. They are strong enough to give each other space, and in so doing, they can know each other better. Gibran also says, "the mountain to the climber is clearer from the plane."

Independence makes interdependence possible. Without a healthy sense of independence, I will love you because I feel deficient in some way. I will love you out of my neediness, not out of the healthy human *need* to love. Erich Fromm made a famous distinction in his book *The Art of Loving*. He asked, "Do you love me because you need me or do you need me because you love me?" None of us are perfect, and there may be some neediness in most all of our love. But the ideal is for me to love you because as a human being it is my nature to love, and therefore I don't love you because I need you (out of my neediness); I need you because I love you, because I'm a human being who needs to love as part of my essence and my very beingness.

The more a couple moves toward the realm of "ours," the more they see each other in a more spontaneous way. It is hard to change an image of someone when you've defined them or their behavior in a certain fixed way. There is a kind of rigid bias that can get lodged in your mind, and when you have such a biased definition, you tend to find data to support your position. These frozen, biased views should be long gone by the time a couple reaches the interdependency stage. Certainly, each partner knows the idiosyncrasies or downright irritating faults of their partner, and there may be some heated fussing at times, but there's always a sense of limits: knowing how far to go and certainly never raging.

THE DEVONS

The Devons are a couple I admire greatly. They were high school sweethearts. Jack was twenty-three and Sharon nineteen when they married. The Devons experienced an initial PRSD jolt a few months after they married. That is when I first met them. They stopped having sex for three weeks. They were disoriented and confused about their "sexual breach" when they first came to see me. Both Jack and Sharon were passionate people. When their romance button turned off, it caught them off guard. After four sessions, they felt grounded again. I had them do some low-risk touching and holding exercises, which helped them get back on track. I saw them from time to time at church on Sunday. We became good friends.

The Devons experienced another PRSD jolt after the birth of their second son. Jack was totally engrossed with his first son. Sharon was concerned that Jack didn't feel the same love and affection for his second son as for their first. Their sex life went into mild PRSD.

Jack and Sharon were both hands-on executives. They both had a high level of testosterone and were used to being in control. This situation caught them by surprise. Their conscious and unconscious anger was being manifested in sexual withholding.

The Devons were extremely honest and docile in terms of learning. We spent several counseling sessions exploring the situation. Jack was enamored with his first child, certainly not uncommon, but after Sharon expressed her feelings, he assured her of his deep commitment to his newborn son. It took six visits with some more assignments of low-risk touch and holding to set them on the right track. The counseling sessions helped them learn how to express their anger toward each other. They'd never had to do that before.

Every year they take a new trip—occasionally repeating one they previously enjoyed a great deal. Jack and Sharon Devon have both been blessed with good health, and they work hard at keeping themselves fit. They love outdoor types of vacations: camping, fishing, even mountain climbing.

Over the years they've ordered academic programs from various sources. They studied them together and shared their insights. Jack and Sharon are students at heart and love to learn and share. The real lesson the Devons can offer every married couple is their shared enthusiasm, energy, and quest for novelty. They have worked hard at keeping themselves full of life, doing new things together.

DOING NOVEL THINGS TOGETHER
IGNITES ROMANCE

As I researched this book, I discovered many studies showing that novelty (doing new things together) can spark romantic passion. I've already stated that the PEA dopamine cocktail is intensified by risk, danger, fear, and adversity. Seeking new experiences that are exciting and slightly risky can be the stimulant that creates passion for another who shares the novel experience with you.

One study by Art Aron and his colleague, Christina Norman, showed that risky and exciting novel activities can actually stimulate *romantic love*. Other studies had already shown that couples who do exciting things find more satisfaction in their relationship. Aron and Norman asked twenty-eight dating and married couples to do two exercises and fill out questionnaires after each one. One exercise was exciting and one was dull. Some couples got the exciting exercises and some got the dull ones. Only the couples who did the exciting exercises experienced feelings of romantic love for their partner.

THE DEVONS' ULTIMATE
NEW ADVENTURE

Shortly after their fortieth anniversary, circumstances led the Devons to adopt a child. Jack was sixty-two and Sharon fifty-eight. The child, a beautiful little girl, was almost one year old when the Devons got her. Jack had always wanted a girl child. Their new daughter initially caused them some distress—her presence created triangles, as each very bright parent argued for the right way to raise her. I recommended they see an expert on parenting with the focus being a girl child. They got to a point of real sharing as parents. Both expressed the feeling that the whole new issue of parenting was a shared conflict that brought them closer together.

Eight years later, Jack told me that, "At seventy, I have a

hard time keeping up with my little girl." But he added, "There's nothing more thrilling than to watch a child grow, and having a little girl all excited to see you when you get home." What was clear to me was that Jack and Sharon's generous spirits had saved a little girl's life. Their new child was neither Jack's nor Sharon's—"She's ours," Jack told me.

On the latest visit I had with the Devons, Jack told me that after forty-nine years of marriage, his and Sharon's sex life was flourishing and that they have a unity and a sharing that is more intimate than ever. Sharon totally agreed. The Devons write a new marriage contract each year one day after their anniversary date. They have renewed their vows and life together every five years in a ritual they jointly create with their Unity Church minister.

POLARITIES AND INTIMACY

The realm of "ours" is exactly *that*—it's not yours or mine; it's ours together. At this stage, couples like the Devons are vulnerable to each other and have hung in there and learned a lot about intimacy. Jack and Sharon have verified a lot of what I believe true intimacy can be. In Chart 12A, "Profile of Intimacy," you can see that intimacy involves a lot of polarities.

PLATEAU INTIMACY

At Stage 3 in our self-generating stages of love, the ecstatic intimacy that we had when we were in-love is gone, but there certainly is or can be what I'd call *plateau intimacy*. The Devons have had moments in their life that they described to me as an "oceanic feeling of oneness." The duration of their togetherness is extremely important. It's the thing you don't have during the in-love romance program. Sharon once told me, "It's important to know we can have conflict and that no one is going to be hurt."

Self-disclosure is the hardest part of intimacy, especially if you've struggled with toxic shame. The very nature of toxic shame is to hide. You don't want anyone to see that you're flawed and defective. After years of loving and working on themselves, and letting each other be, toxic shame usually goes away.

ACCOUNTABILITY AND NEGOTIABILITY

Accountability is always part of an intimate relationship. I am responsible to my spouse, and I'm responsible for what I've done. But our relationship is also negotiable. From time to time we may not want to do the same things, and it's important that we can respect each other and negotiate, and not take each other for granted.

Chart 12A:
Profile of Intimacy

Intimacy involves a number of polarities:

Ecstasy	Duration
Moments of extreme oneness due to our "in-love" program, especially our amazing sex.	Enough time to test and trust each other. Time allows a couple to grow in their knowledge of self and of each other.
Emotive Warmth	**Conflict Capability**
Good feelings about being loved and about being kind, generous, and nurturing to our partner.	The trust and honesty necessary to express anger and resentments with effective, pro-active communication skills.
Courage of Self-Disclosure	**Letting Be**
Allowing the other to know us as we really are. The docility to learn how to show our vulnerability to our partner.	Being the custodians of each other's solitude and privacy.
Accountability	**Negotiability**
Having a sense of duty to the other person; being accountable to him/her for our time and behavior.	Being able to negotiate our own private interests, activities, and growth needs.

"I CAN'T LIVE WITHOUT YOU"

In short, in a "good enough" intimate relationship, one person loves the other because of the perceived desirability of the other in their very beingness. One should shy away from loving a person because he or she fills the subjective voids in the desirer. In that situation, one is drawn to the other as a way to complete oneself. "I can't live without you," is a dangerous, co-dependent statement. Two incomplete half-people never make a whole. The calling of the spouse as "my better half," a common statement from the past, is a grossly misleading statement. One-half times one-half equals *one-fourth*! And that's not far from the fact that 17 percent of the 50 percent who stay married feel diminished. Each gets a fourth of what they could be getting. "I don't *want* to live without you," is a healthier way to express oneself.

THE RANGE OF INTIMACY

People frequently think of intimacy only in terms of romance and sex. Those are certainly intense and beautiful areas of intimacy, but intimacy is not limited to sex and romance! Look at Chart 12B, "The Range of Intimacy." I've listed twelve activities that couples can share. I think of my spouse and I raising our children; about how we worried (literally shared worry) about our children. These were times of deep sharing, and they brought us together. Take a look at the list, and I'll bet some memories come floating in.

Chart 12B: The Range of Intimacy

The range of intimate sharing is as large as the possibilities of relating. Some of the more common forms of intimacy are:

- Emotional (empathy or empathetic listening)
- Recreational (having fun and playing together)
- Sexual (erotic or orgasmic closeness)
- Intellectual (sharing the world of ideas)
- Work (sharing common tasks)
- Aesthetic (sharing the experience of beauty)
- Creative (sharing acts of creating together)
- Crisis (coping with problems and pain)
- Commitment (mutually derived from common self-interest)
- Spiritual (sharing ultimate concerns)
- Communication (the source of all types of intimacy)
- Conflict (learning about each other as we reveal ourselves in conflict)

LONELINESS VERSUS SOLITUDE

It's important to see that intimacy is not desirable all the time. There needs to be some solitude in human life. Solitude is not loneliness. Loneliness is a trait of those who are unfulfilled, those with various degrees of unresolved issues from the past. In fact, wholeness demands solitude, because in solitude, each person experiences his or her own selfness. This separation also allows us to see some of the truly unique traits of the other. We need distance to see each other's unique selfhood (the otherness of the other). We need distance to keep from becoming lost in familiarity.

FAMILIARITY BREEDS CONTEMPT

As a couple, two whole people seek out new things, learn new things, and have adventures. This keeps the relationship from becoming toxically familiar. The philosopher Hegel said, "A thing in so far as it is familiar is unknown." Couples who get caught up in neediness and enmeshment get stuck. They are like two people in a canoe; when one moves one way, the other moves the same way. They become familiar, take each other for granted, and fear change in their partner. On the other hand, a healthy familiarity allows each partner to feel safe with the other.

RESENTMENT AND FORGIVENESS

Two highly individuated people are not petty; they are committed to growth. They are willing to forgive, because holding on to resentments keep them stuck. Resentment is from the French *resentire*, which means to refeel. A resentment is a re-feeling of the same thing over and over again. It is a terrible rut. Forgiveness is for the person forgiving, because it releases them from the energy that it takes to hold on to the resentment. They are no longer bound to the past. Strong people forgive more easily, while weak people find it difficult. Start your slates clean today!

EPILOGUE

IF I HOLD YOU IN MY HEART YOU'LL WITHER;
BECOME A THORN IF I HOLD YOU IN MY EYES.
NO, I'LL MAKE A PLACE FOR YOU WITHIN MY SOUL INSTEAD;
SO YOU'LL BE MY LOVE IN LIVES BEYOND THIS LIFE.

—Rumi

At the end of our lives, the two most important things will be: (1) who we loved, and (2) how fully we lived our lives. That is the meaning of the African proverb that says, "When death finds you, hope that it finds you alive." I can think of nothing worse than going to my death and never knowing who I was. What will our legacy statement be? Do we have a sense of our destiny and/or some sense of our unique, divine incarnation?

Certainly we want our lifework to be part of our legacy, but it seems to me that our most sacred moments are the "I and thou" moments with our spouses, children, and friends—but especially with our spouses. Loving each other day by day, being willing to continue the cherishing behaviors, we know our spouse's love is a little bit of heaven on earth.

In *The Soul of Sex*, author Thomas Moore says that, "in a relationship the divine has the upper hand." Certainly, our most cherished love relationship is a *mystery* to be lived. And certainly, as the Catholic mystic John of the Cross said, "In the evening of life, we will be judged on love alone."

ACKNOWLEDGMENTS

I wish to acknowledge all the people I've especially referred to in the text of this book. I unconditionally recommend their work. I must especially acknowledge Dr. Helen Fisher, Dr. Pat Carnes, Dr. Pat Love, Dr. Harriet Lerner, Dr. Jeffrey Schwartz, Dr. Claudia Black, Dr. John Gottman, Richard Bandler, John Grinder, Leslie Cameron Bandler, and Dr. Murray Bowen.

I have special friendships with Pia Mellody, Johnny Lee, Dr. Claudia Black, and Dr. Pat Carnes. Pat, Claudia, and I have presented workshops together and have had self-expanding discussions. Pia is retired now, but she and I are senior fellows at The Meadows treatment center. Pia was an inspiration to me in developing my Inner Child Workshop. Pat Carnes has been the creative source for the whole sexual recovery movement.

I also wish to acknowledge my other senior fellows, A. Bissel van der Kolk, Peter Levine, Dr. Shelley Uram, and Dr. Jon Caldwell at The Meadows treatment center in Wickenburg, Arizona, who are world pioneers in treating trauma. Enormous praise goes to Jim Dredge, who has transformed The Meadows into the best treatment center in the world. To Carrie Steffensen, who brilliantly set up and managed workshops for me for the last fourteen years. She also took care of my travel and comfort needs in an extraordinarily nurturing way. She is kind, loving, and brilliant!

I must also thank my wife, Karen Ann Bradshaw, and my son, John, for their frank and sometimes jolting feedback. Karen has been a behind-the-scenes resource person and has had to put up with my overinflated, narcissistic wounds for nineteen years. She is an amazing woman in every way!

A special thanks goes to my publisher, Peter Vegso. He is an extraordinary businessman and is very kind, insightful, sensitive, and patient. Pray that the ringing in his ears stop! Thanks also to Gary Seidler, who has always supported me. The entire staff of Health Communications are the very best!

I want to especially acknowledge my editor, Christine Belleris, who helped make this a better book. I cannot possibly express my gratitude to Carrie Renard Stocker (soon to be a brilliant nurse) who aided me in the preparation of the manuscript for this book. Carrie amazed me with her unbelievably fast typing and her willingness to work anytime of the day or night (while taking her difficult nursing exams).

I also wish to thank my seven-year-old daughter, Ariel, who sat on my desk as well as my shoulders, urging me "to finish the book, Papa, so you can play with me!" And finally, I'm grateful for our new dog, Chase Marley Bradshaw, who sat faithfully by my desk and tried to eat my manuscript (some days I wish he had).

RESOURCES

I'm sincerely grateful to the following, whose work I have quoted in this book.

Bandler, Richard and John Grinder. *Frogs into Princes: Neuro Linguistic Programming.* Moab, UT: Real People Press, 1979.

Bowen, Murray. *Family Therapy in Clinical Practice.* Lanham, MD: Jason Arnson, Inc., 1993.

Bradshaw, John. *Bradshaw On: The Family: A New Way of Creating Solid Self Esteem.* Deerfield Beach, FL.: Health Communications, Inc., 1990.

___. *Creating Love: The Next Stage of Growth.* New York: Bantam Books, 1994.

___. *Healing the Shame That Binds You.* Deerfield Beach, FL: Health Communications, Inc., 2005.

___. *Homecoming: Reclaiming and Championing Your Inner Child.* New York: Bantam Books, 1992.

Cancian, Francesca. *Love in America: Gender and Self-Development.* New York: Cambridge University Press, 1990.

Carnes, Patrick. *Out of the Shadows: Understanding Sexual Addiction.* Center City, MN: Hazelden Publishing, 2001.

Carnes, Patrick and Joseph Moriarity. *Sexual Anorexia.* Center City, MN: Hazelden Publishing, 2004.

Fisher, Helen. *Why We Love: The Nature and Chemistry of Romantic Love.* New York: Holt Paperbacks, 2004.

___. *Anatomy of Love: A Natural History of Mating, Marriage and Why We Stay Together.* New York: Ballantine Books, 1994.

Gallup, Gordan, Rebecca Burch and Steven Platek. "Does Semen Have Antidepressant Properties?" *Archives of Sexual Behavior,* 13 (26), 289-293, 2003.

Gottman, John. *The Seven Principles for Making Marriage Work: A Guide from the Country's Foremost Relationship Expert.* New York: The Crown Publishing Group, 2000.

___. *What Predicts Divorce? The Relationship Between Marital Processes and Marital Outcomes.* New York: Psychology Press, 1993.

Greenberg, Mark, Dante Cicchetti, and E. Mark Cummings. *Attachment in the Preschool Years: Theory, Research, and Intervention.* Chicago: University of Chicago Press, 1990.

Lerner, Harriet. *The Dance of Intimacy: A Woman's Guide to Courageous Acts of Change in Key Relationships.* New York: Harper Perennial, 1997.

Love, Patricia. *The Truth About Love: The Highs, the Lows, and How You Can Make it Last Forever.* New York: Touchstone, 2001.

Mellody, Pia. *Facing Love Addiction: Giving Yourself the Power to Change the Way You Love.* New York: HarperOne 2003.

___. *The Intimacy Factor: The Ground Rules for Overcoming the Obstacles to Truth, Respect, and Lasting Love.* New York: HarperOne, 2004.

Nathanson, Donald. *Shame and Pride: Affect, Sex, and the Birth of the Self.* New York: W. W. Norton & Company, Inc., 1992.

Schwartz, Jeffrey, with Sharon Begley. *The Mind and the Brain: Neuroplasticity and the Power of Mental Force.* New York: Regan Books, 2003.

Whyte, David. See *http://www.davidwhyte.com.*

RECOMMENDED RESOURCES FOR FURTHER ENRICHMENT

Ainsworth, Mary, Blehar, Mary C. and Everett Waters. *Patrons of Attachment: A Psychological Study of the Strange Situation.* New York: Psychology Press, 2014.

Bandler, Leslie. *They Lived Happily Ever After: Methods for Achieving Happy Endings in Coupling.* Capitola, CA: Meta Publications, 1978.

Begly, Sharon. *Train Your Mind, Change Your Brain: How a New Science Reveals our Extraordinary Potential to Change Ourselves.* New York: Ballantine Books, 2007.

Berg, S.J. and K.E. Wynne-Edwards. *Changes in testosterone, cortisol, and estradiol levels in men becoming fathers.* 76(6) (2001): 582–92.

Black, Claudia. *Deceived: Facing Sexual Betrayal, Lies, and Secrets.* Center City, MN: Hazelden Publishing, 2009.

Bowlby, John. *A Secure Base: Parent-Child Attachment and Healthy Human Development.* New York: Basic Books, 1988.

Bradshaw, John. *Family Secrets: The Path from Shame to Healing.* New York: Bantam Books, 1996.

___. *Reclaiming Virtue: How We Can Develop the Moral Intelligence to Do the Right Thing at the Right Time for the Right Reason.* New York: Bantam Books, 2009.

Buber, Martin. *I and Thou.* New York: Touchstone, 1971.

Campbell, Susan. *The Couples Journey: Intimacy as a Path to Wholeness.* Atascadero, CA: Impact Publishers, 1980.

Canning, Maureen. *Lust, Anger, Love: Understanding Sexual Addiction and The Road to Healthy Intimacy.* Naperville, IL: Sourcebooks, 2008.

Catlett, Joyce and Robert Firestone. *Fear of Intimacy.* Washington, DC: American Psychological Association, 1999.

Covington, Stephanie. *Awakening Your Sexuality: A Guide for Recovering Women.* San Francisco: Harper San Francisco, 1992.

Coontz, Stephanie. *Marriage, a History: How Love Conquered Marriage.* New York: Penguin Books, 2006.

___. *The Way We Never Were: American Families and the Nostalgia Trap.* New York: Basic Books, 1993.

Covitz, Joel. *Emotional Child Abuse: The Family Curse.* Salem, MA: Sigo Press, 1986.

Damasio, Antonio. *Descartes Error: Emotion, Reason, and the Human Brain.* New York: Penguin Book, 2005.

___. *The Feelings of What Happens: Body and Emotion in the Making of Consciousness.* Boston, MA: Mariner Books, 2000.

Ellis, Havelock. *Studies in the Psychology of Sex, Volume 1—The Evolution of Modesty; The Phenomena of Sexual Periodicity; Auto-Erotism.* Ontario: Ontario Classic Books, 2010.

Darwin, Charles. *The Expressions of Emotions in Man and Animals.* New York: CreateSpace Independent Publishing Platform, 2012.

Doidge, Normon. *The Brain That Changes Itself: Stories of Personal Triumph from the Frontiers of Brain Science.* New York: Penguin Books, 2007.

Erikson, Erik H. *Insight and Responsibility.* New York: W. W. Norton & Company, Inc., 1994.

___. *Childhood and Society.* New York: W. W. Norton & Company, Inc., 1993.

Farber, Leslie. *The Ways of the Will: Selected Essays Expanded Edition.* New York: Basic Books, 2000.

Firestone, Robert. *The Fantasy Bond: Structure of Psychological Defenses.* Santa Barbara, CA: Glendon Association, 1987.

Fosha, Diane. *The Transforming Power of Affect: A Model for Accelerating Change.* New York: Basic Books, 2000.

Fromm, Erich. *The Art of Loving.* New York: Harper Perennial Modern Classics, 2006.

Haley, Jay. *Uncommon Therapy: The Psychiatric Techniques of Milton H. Ericson, M.D.* New York: W. W. Norton & Company, Inc., 1993.

Hastings, Anne S. *Discovering Sexuality That Will Satisfy You Both: When Couples Want Different Amounts and Different Kinds of Sex.* Novato, CA: Printed Voice, 1993.

Hendrix, Harville. *Getting the Love You Want: A Guide for Couples, 20th Anniversary Addition.* New York: Henry Holt & Co., 2007.

Hillman, James. *The Soul's Code: In Search of Character and Calling.* New York: Grand Central Publishing, 1997.

Hoffman, Bob. *No One Is to Blame: Freedom from Compulsive Self-Defeating Behavior; The Discoveries of the Quadrinity Process.* Palo Alto, CA: Science and Behavior Books, Inc., 1988.

Hollis, James. *Finding Meaning in the Second Half of Life: How to Finally, Really Grow Up.* New York: Gotham Books, 2006.

___. *Hauntings: Dispelling the Ghosts Who Run Our Lives.* Asheville, NC: Chiron Publications, 2013.

Jackson, Don and William Lederer. *The Mirages of Marriage.* New York: W. W. Norton & Company, Inc., 1968.

Kassorla, Irene. *Putting it All Together: The New Orthomolecular Nutrition.* Columbus, OH: McGraw-Hill, 1998.

Kriegman, Daniel and Malcolm Slavin. *The Adaptive Design of the Human Psyche: Psychoanalysis, Evolutionary Biology, and the Therapeutic Process.* New York: Guilford Press, 1992.

Ledoux. *The Emotional Brain: The Mysterious Underpinnings of Emotional Life.* New York: Simon and Schuster, 1998.

Lee, John. *The Anger Solution: The Proven Method for Achieving Calm and Developing Healthy, Long-Lasting Relationships.* Jackson, TN: Da Capo Press, 2009.

Levine, Peter and Ann Federick. *Walking the Tiger: Healing Trauma.* Berkeley, CA: North Atlantic Books, 1997.

Liebowitz, Michael MD. *The Chemistry of Love.* New York: Penguin, 1955.

Lowen, Alexander. *The Journal of Sex Research Vol. 4.* New York: Taylor and Francis, 1968.

Middleton-Moz, Jane. *Children of Trauma: Rediscovering Your Discarded Self.* Deerfield Beach, FL: Health Communications, Inc., 1989.

Moore, Thomas. *The Soul of Sex: Cultivating Life as an Act of Love.* New York: Harper Perennial, 1999.

Pastor, Marion. *Anger and Forgiveness: An Approach That Works.* Berkeley, CA: Jennis Press, 1990.

Peck, Scott. *The Road Less Traveled: A New Psychology of Love, Traditional Values and Spiritual Growth.* New York: Simon and Schuster, 2003.

Pletcher, Claudine and Sally Bartolameolli. *Relationships from Addiction to Authenticity: Understanding Co-Sex Addiction–A Spiritual Journey to Wholeness and Serenity.* Deerfield Beach, FL: Health Communications, Inc., 2008.

Satir, Virginia. *Conjoint Family Therapy.* Palo Alto, CA: Science and Behavior Books, 1983.

Scheler, Max. Über Scham ünd Schamgefühl—to French: *La Pudeur.* Paris: Aubier, 1952.

Schnarch, David. *Intimacy and Desire: Awaken the Passion in Your Relationship.* New York: Beaufort Books, 2011.

Schneider, Carl. *Shame, Exposure and Privacy.* New York: W. W. Norton & Company, Inc., 1992.

Schore, Allan. *Affect Regulation and the Repair of the Self.* New York: W. W. Norton & Company, Inc., 2003.

___. *Affect Dysregulation and Disorders of the Self.* New York: W. W. Norton & Company, Inc., 2003.

Van der Kolk, Bessel A. *Traumatic Stress: The Effects of Overwhelming Experience of Mind, Body, and Society.* New York: Guilford Press, 1996.

Watzlawick, Paul and John Weakland. *Change: Principles of Problem Formation and Problem Resolution.* New York: W. W. Norton & Co., 2011.

Wegscheider-Cruse. *Choicemaking: For Spirituality Seekers, Co-Dependents and Adult Children.* Deerfield Beach, FL: Health Communications, Inc., 1986.

Whitfield, Charles. *Healing the Child Within: Discovery and Recovery for Adult Children of Dysfunctional Families.* Deerfield Beach, FL: Health Communications, Inc., 1987.

Wolinsky, Stephen. *Trances People Live.* Ashley Falls, MA: Bramble Co., 1991.

ABOUT THE AUTHOR

For more than forty-eight years, **John Bradshaw** has combined the roles of counselor, author, theologian, management consultant, public speaker, and teacher, becoming one of the leading figures in the fields of addiction/recovery and family systems.

Born in Houston, Texas, into a troubled family and abandoned by his alcoholic father, John became an academic overachiever and an out-of-control teenager. He studied for the Roman Catholic priesthood at a seminary run by the religious order of St. Basil, where he remained for nine years, leaving just prior to being ordained. During this time he earned degrees in psychology and theology from the University of Toronto. It was also during this time that a high school drinking problem became a full-fledged addiction.

On December 11, 1965, John took a drastic step—he committed himself to Austin State Hospital. After six days he signed himself out of the hospital and entered an alcohol recovery program. Soon afterward he began to lecture at a local church and before long was in demand as a teacher, counselor, speaker, and corporate consultant.

In 1986, with the airing of *Bradshaw On: The Family*, John became a public television phenomenon, with a total of six public television series and two specials that reached millions of viewers. In 1996, he also appeared on national network TV in his syndicated talk show, *The Bradshaw Difference*. Through this period he also gave talks and multiday workshops attended by thousands of people at a time.

His previous books include *Bradshaw On: The Family* (a *New York Times* bestseller), *Healing the Shame That Binds You* (a #2 *New York Times* bestseller), *Homecoming* (a #1 *New York Times* bestseller), *Creating Love* (a #1 *New York Times* bestseller), *Family Secrets*, and *Reclaiming Virtue*.

He is currently a senior fellow at The Meadows, a leading addiction treatment center in Wickenburg, Arizona, and makes presentations nationwide on the inner child and *feeling* work he pioneered. Before he joined The Meadows, John founded The John Bradshaw Center at Ingleside Hospital, which he oversaw for ten years.

The father of four children and stepchildren and grandfather of three, he resides in Houston, Texas, with his wife, Karen Ann. He has become a true elder who has personally guided some half-million participants in his unique healing work, and whose bestselling books and TV series have reached many millions more throughout the world. In 2001, the editors and readers of *Common Boundary* magazine named John one of the one hundred most influential writers on psychology and spirituality in the twentieth century.

John conducts lectures and workshops throughout the world. For information about upcoming lectures, workshops, and keynote addresses, or to purchase CDs or DVDs of John's workshops or lecture series, including his PBS series, please visit *www.johnbradshaw.com.*

Within the United States: 800-6-BRADSHAW

Outside the United States: 713-771-1300

Facsimile: 713-771-1362

To contact John Bradshaw:

John Bradshaw
PO Box 667147
Houston, TX 77266-7147

or

youcanheal@aol.com

INDEX

Note: a *c* denotes a chart; an *f* denotes a figure.